WHATEVER HAPPENED TO THE ANIMALS OF NOAH'S ARK?

© Rev. Robert J. Kraig

All rights reserved. No part of this publication may be reproduced, stored in a retrieval system, or transmitted in any form or by any means, electronic, mechanical, photocopying, recording, or otherwise, without the prior written permission of the author or the publisher.

ISBN 0-9661937-2-5

Library of Congress Catalog Card Number 99-96321

Printed in the United States of America

FIRST EDITION

Published by:

ASHCO PUBLICATIONS, INC.
P.O. Box 3006
Ashtabula, OH 44005-3066

CONTENTS

Dedication.. i

Acknowledgements.. ii

Introduction... iii

Chapter 1—The Rabbit....................................... 1

Chapter 2—The Kangaroo.................................. 13

Chapter 3—The Dog... 27

Chapter 4—The Raccoon.................................... 41

Chapter 5—The Badger...................................... 53

Chapter 6—The Hyena....................................... 67

Chapter 7—The Skunk....................................... 79

Chapter 8—The Zebra.. 93

Chapter 9—The Squirrel..................................... 107

Chapter 10—The Pelican.................................... 119

Summary.. 133

Novena... 139

DEDICATION

Dedicated to all those I have encountered in my ministry who provided me with the growth I have experienced; and especially to my mother, sister, and my father whom I know is celebrating the great gift of eternal life.

Proceeds from this book will go to the Priest Infirm Fund of the Diocese of Cleveland, Our Lady of the Wayside Home, and Make a Wish Foundation.

ACKNOWLEDGEMENTS

To all those who have helped me realize the various animals within myself during my 27 years as a priest, I say thank you. And to all of those who continue to live and minister with me, as I continue to recognize these animals in my own life, I especially give thanks.

I am especially grateful to my brother priests, David Trask, Tim Gareau, Bob Wisniewski, Peter Mihalic, To Sr. Pat Sylvester and Sr. Mary Popoczy, both Sisters of Notre Dame; Dr. John Radkowski, a marriage counselor, who has helped me reach out to many couples, and to Mr. Jack Borkey, Sr., president of PEPCO, for all their help and encouragement in getting my thoughts down on paper. And a special word of thanks to Fr. Jim Stenger for helping to develop my ideas and whose friendship and support continues to keep me a priest. Finally thanks to my nephew, Brian Neuman, whose love for the outdoors, animals and camping was invaluable to me.

Scripture selections are taken from the New American Bible with Revised New Testament Copyright © 1986, 1970 by the Confraternity of Christian Doctrine, 3211 Fourth St., N.E., Washington, D.C. 20017-1194 and are used by license of the copyright owner. All rights reserved. No part of the New American Bible may be reproduced in any form without permission in writing from the copyright owner.

INTRODUCTION

One of my favorite stories of Jesus and the Last Supper is when Jesus takes His apostles out to a fancy, upscale restaurant to eat the last meal with them. As you well know, when you eat a meal with good friends there comes a time in the meal when you sit back, relax, have a fresh cup of coffee and just enjoy the company of those around you. When you are with good friends, whom you have shared life, joys, sufferings, challenges and Jesus, it is a special time to be in the presence of one another.

As the story goes Jesus reached that time of the meal. But he looked around and saw the crew he had with him. He saw Peter and said: "Peter, how could you ever be the one to deny me three times? I made you head of this group, trusted you, entrusted many sacred moments to you and you are going to deny me!"

To Matthew, "And Matthew, how could you take advantage of so many people with that tax collecting of yours? To think you 'stuck it' to so many who were unable to pay!"

And to Nathaniel, "Nathaniel, how could you ever be so rude and ask the question, 'Can any good come from Nazareth?'"

And to Judas, "And you, Judas, to think you would betray me! Why? What did I ever do to you to deserve that?"

To Thomas, "And, Thomas, after being with you all this time, to think you would doubt me!"

And finally to James and John, "And you two, I'm sick and tired of your mom always asking me 'can they have special seats in the Kingdom of God?' If she does that one more time I'm going to lose it!"

At that moment the waiter came around with the check, a rather exorbitant amount to say the least. And, as the story goes, Jesus, after viewing the boys around him, glanced at the check, looked at the waiter and simply said, "Waiter, separate checks, please!"

Not one of us, no matter what our walk of life, our failings, our weaknesses or sinfulness, have ever experienced Jesus giving us separate checks. In fact he took the whole bill. He gave His life for us, sent His Spirit to guide us and finally blest us with the promise of eternal life. How cherished we are that our God would be willing to do this for us.

And yet, any of us, whether Peter, Judas, Nathaniel, Matthew, James, John, or whomever have failed to rightly understand the message of God and His Kingdom. The truth of the matter is that whenever people gather, (whether in the parish, at work, recreation or vacation,) no two personalities are the same. In the presence of the divergent backgrounds, gifts, talents, issues, personalities and resources, the presence of God becomes REAL.

Twenty-seven years into parish ministry the Lord moved me to reflect on the personalities within a faith community; personalities for which He suffered, died and rose from the dead. This inspiration came one morning, about 3:00 a.m., when I awoke to the question: 'Whatever happened to the animals after they came off Noah's ark?'

I have chosen to write about ten animals that came off the ark: The rabbit, zebra, raccoon, badger, dog, hyena, skunk, squirrel, kangaroo and the pelican. And more than just writing about the animals, but speaking of their personification within the life of a faith community.

There is definitely a dark side to each of the animals about which I will be writing as I take you through the "zoo." However, I hope to show the redemptive side that reveals the presence of God in our lives, our places of worship, and our places of employment.

The main reason for this journey is because each of the animals I have experienced the last twenty-seven years has convinced me of this -- neither an individual nor a faith community will grow, or remain viable, unless it is centered around the Body and Blood of Christ, and around prayer. With such a focus, our perspective, our issues, our emphasis, our lives and our communities change—radically.

There are a lot of animals within our faith communities. I often say, "It's the same zoo everywhere, just different animals!" Every weekend when we gather to celebrate the life, death and resurrection of Jesus (and even during the week when we gather), there is a motley crew of animals present—including the priest celebrant. This zoo has helped me grow and has driven me to my knees in prayer. Hopefully my prayerful reflections inspire others, so they can feed me, so I can nourish them.

This book is not written to poke fun or to ridicule. I believe I criticize in others those weaknesses and faults I do not like about myself. The animals about which I have chosen to write reflect qualities in individuals who have given me insight into myself. What may be perceived as ridicule, criticism or venting of frustration is actually gratitude—gratitude to those who have helped me realize something more about myself and the animals that are within me. Throughout this book I hope to share how the weaknesses I have come to recognize, have provided tremendous growth for me and the Priesthood in which I share.

As we begin our walk through the zoo, be mindful that this book is not a theological treatise on priesthood, parish ministry, Church or the Eucharist. It is simply a reflection by a parish priest.

We only have each other, family, friends, parish communities, fellow workers. If we're in the zoo it is necessary to learn to live with one another, to rejoice in each other's gifts, to learn from our failures and to celebrate life together. Yes, we only do have each other, but all of us together have the love and forgiveness of God which we share together in our liturgical prayer.

In the end it may be difficult for some to believe, but there is only one thing we must trust about our God, HE DOES NOT

ABANDON US! We all come with parts of the animals described in this book and it is good for me to be a part of the zoo. I am certainly one with traits of those animals within me; but, as I said, it is good to be part of the zoo.

As we journey through the zoo remember that all names used are fictitious. The examples, however, come from lived experiences. All Scripture references are from The New American Bible.

I have often said that the power of God is so real, and the fact that St. John Neumann parish is still growing in the Lord after almost ten years of me as pastor, proves the power of God. That power of God is in all of us. Despite who we are and what animal we are, God continues to touch people through each and every one of us. In the end we can only say this about the zoo: Praise God!

CHAPTER 1

THE RABBIT

A man was looking for the most beautiful woman in the world. While out taking a stroll one day he noticed the 'girl of his dreams!' "Ah," he said, "at last—the one I've been looking for all my life." She then proceeded to tell him that another beautiful woman was walking behind him. When he turned around she quickly started to move away. "Wait", he said, "you're the girl I've been looking for!" To which she responded, "If I was the most beautiful girl in the world then why did you turn around?"

The rabbit, similar to the man in the above story, is symbolic of our culture that encourages us to move from one fad to another.
- What's in style one season is out the next.
- Buy a computer and six months later there's a new and better one being advertised.
- During the season of Christmas, last year's prime toy is passed over for something new.

We quickly move, or in terms of the rabbit, "hop" from one thing to another. Because our culture is perpetually in flux, we need a solid foundation in our lives to give meaning, focus and purpose.

In parish life, I would classify a rabbit as one who moves from parish to parish, from here to there, always looking for: the perfect parish, perfect priest, perfect pastoral associate, or perfect organization. The person with rabbit characteristics believes he has found the perfect environment, only to become disillusioned because there is no foundation in his life. The rabbit is quick to turn from prayer and the Eucharist, (which are nurtured through rootedness) and hop to another locality to meet his or her perceived needs.

Thus the fad of society can be transitioned to parish life when a rabbit is enthralled by one of the church's ministers or organizations. A rabbit is tempted to say something like, "Father Joe, when you say mass I think I see Jesus Himself!" Or, "The way you hold the host at the consecration, Father, moves me to tears."

The rabbit also manifests itself in:

- "Father, you have such a lovely voice—when you sing I think I'm in heaven with the choir of angels!"
- "Sister, I don't know where we'd be without you—we're so lucky to have you!"
- Or, "Father, you're the best thing that ever came to this parish."

Since the rabbit's statements are very complimentary and the rabbit is a fairly innocent animal, one can justly ask how this type of person can be a detriment to parish life. After all, rabbits are cute furry creatures that are found throughout the United States and beyond.

When I jog around our parish grounds I occasionally see a rabbit. I wish it would stay in one place so I could go up and start conversing with it. But when I come within a few feet, it quickly moves away. So again: why is the person, who is so affirming, called a rabbit? The statements they make are certainly positive ones. Unfortunately, however, they can also be very ego inflating. A current phenomenon is the radio talk show. People call in with various opinions on any given topic. Sometimes these shows are interesting and I believe they give people the opportunity to vent their feelings. It is amazing how one can be praised one day and criticized another. It's that kind of play that goes on within the rabbit. What pleases him one day may not please him the following. As a result, its hippity hop to another parish. Let me explain.

On one day the rabbits believe they have found the perfect parish. The priest, minister, music and organizations simply are the best. Then, however, Father 'Perfectamundo' says something from the pulpit they do not agree with or something happens which they feel is not a part of their notion of church. So, they hop to another parish. It may be something like girl servers coming out to minister, women lectoring at a Sunday liturgy, all the ciboria were not on the corporal, or some devotion they do not embrace. Regardless, the rabbits immediately hop away.

At the next parish it may be an innocent remark in a homily, a comment about the role of Mary in salvation history, the placement of the tabernacle in the church, a church with kneelers or without them or the quoting of an author whom the rabbit does not like. When any or all of these happen, suddenly Sister isn't the best religious teacher or Father isn't perfect. Because the rabbit's foundation is what he or she believes is essential to the church and opposite to the community's prayer and celebration of Eucharist, he or she will hop to another parish.

And the cycle begins again—and once the new Father "Perfectamundo" says something contrary to its beliefs—it's hippity hop, hop, hop, to another parish.

And the cycle repeats itself.

I mentioned that when out jogging, I would like to stop and talk to the rabbit, but, as I approach, it quickly runs. Unfortunately,

after rabbits get upset and hop to another parish, they invest themselves in the new parish no more deeply than they had in the last. Often one finds out what they are angry about and why they moved through some other person. In many ways what the rabbit does in the parish is no different from what the rabbit does in everyday life or in the work world. The rabbit perceives the grass is always greener on the other side of the fence:
- "If I get that promotion then everything will work itself out!"
- "Once we move from this neighborhood things will change!"
- "As soon as we get away on vacation our marriage will be better!"

All these are quick fixes, addressing symptoms but not addressing key problems. While all present us with a "greener picture," the key issue for the rabbit is that there is no firm faith foundation in his life. In a way the rabbit might be similar to the man in the opening story.

For the Christian in parish life, that foundation is the presence of God in our life and in the lives of others. While a rabbit burroughs itself for protection from what is around it, one must take every precaution not to close his or her eyes to the reality of the life within his parish community. It would be nice if life were to progress the way we think it should. You and I both know, however, that it just isn't that way!

If I were to say what keeps me a priest, I would say it is the faith of God's people. Although the rabbit is complimentary, the people who have let go to God keep me in the ministry. Things may appear better on the other side of the fence for them, but their commitment to God, His people and His church are more important than anything else.

In the early nineties, one week before Thanksgiving, a couple from the parish lost their five-year-old son in a car accident and buried him the Tuesday before Thanksgiving. At the Thanksgiving Day Mass, after reaching the presidential chair, I saw this same couple coming down the aisle to celebrate Eucharist, just two days after they buried their son. I thought to myself, what the heck are they doing here—they just buried their son—how can they celebrate Thanksgiving? Then I realized it was their faith—their faith in Eucharist, their faith in the Body of Christ. Having lost their only child, it was important for them to pray with God's people and to strengthen their hope and trust in God's promise to never abandon His people.

Cannot the same be said of so many of our ancestors, so many people today? How many have remained loyal to their commitments to raise families in spite of difficult times? How many have continued to sacrifice for their children and spouses? How many in the past gave us the buildings in which we foster community and minister? They were passed to us only because of our ancestors' commitment to Jesus Christ and faith in His Word!

The kind of family described above, and those mentioned in the preceding paragraph, do not hop from parish to parish looking for the perfect parish, priest or pastoral minister. They know their strength and hope only come from the Body and the Blood of Jesus and the prayer of a community of believers gathered around the Table of the Lord. They understand the fullness of revelation was not revealed to one person or one parish. More important, they realize that Jesus came to redeem our sinfulness and to help us grow in the Kingdom of God. They believe in the ritual of Eucharist, a ritual which involves the community of believers who comprise the Body of Christ in today's world. Just as Jesus, who, in showing us His humanity allowed His divinity to emerge, so we too, as we gather around The Table of the Lord, come with our human condition and allow the Holy One to touch us and to emerge in our life. In celebrating Eucharist, we see Jesus is with us always.

"Can a mother forget her infant,/ be without tenderness for the child of her womb?/ Even should she forget,/ I will never forget you./ See, upon the palms of my hands I have written your name;" (Isaiah 49:15:16a)

As we root our lives in the Word of God that has been enfleshed through the Eucharist and prayer of the community, not only does the individual grow, but, so too, does the entire Body of Christ. The prayer of the community nourishes us as we join hands with others. We become Eucharist to one another.

Neither tragedy nor unforeseen circumstances can lead people of faith away from God's Word and His promise not to abandon us. And because of that conviction, their faith can only bear fruit and touch the lives of others.

Have rabbits reached that level of faith? By not staying around and hopping from one experience to another, how can they find any depth? A depth to root themselves in, and a depth to hear the words of the kingdom which are essential to one's growth!

> "Everyone who listens to those words of mine and acts on them will be like a wise man who built his house on rock. The rain fell, the floods came, and the winds blew and buffeted the house. But it did not collapse; it had been set solidly on rock. And everyone who listens to these words of mine but does not act on them will be like a fool who built his house on sand. The rain fell, the floods came, and the winds blew and buffeted the house. And it collapsed and was completely ruined." (Mt. 7:24-27)

In addition to my own faith being made stronger by God's people, the faith of those who have the courage to confront me about a decision of mine (with which they disagree) also strengthens me. Rather than hop to another parish, their faith keeps them coming to share Eucharist with their faith community. Jesus and the Body of Christ are more important than the actions of any individual. The redemptive side of the rabbit is they help us understand that the fullness of church, the fullness of Christ, the fullness of Eucharist is not found in any one person; it is discovered when the community gathers together to celebrate liturgy. It is at worship when we see the gifts and talents of all assembled, the faith of all present, that Jesus can become visible.

> "There are a different kind of spiritual gifts but the same Spirit; there are different forms of service but the same Lord; there are different workings but the same God who produces all of them in everyone. To each individual the manifestation of the Spirit is given for some benefit. To one is given through the Spirit the expression of wisdom; to another the expression of knowledge according to the same Spirit; to another faith by the same Spirit; to another gifts of healing by the one Spirit; to another mighty deeds; to another prophecy; to another discernment of spirits; to another varieties of tongues; to another interpretation of tongues. But one and the same Spirit produces all of these, distributing them individually to each person as he wishes." (1Cor. 12:4-11)

A rabbit, because he or she has the gift of faith and believes in Jesus, has a great deal to offer the community. As a result, it is a great loss when the rabbit gets upset and hops to another community because they disagree with a person or an organization. And not only do they have much to give to a community; they also have much to receive. God's ways are mysterious, for He often speaks to us through others. In fact, people often find God through the assistance of those whose spirituality is different from theirs. It is difficult to comprehend the logic of the rabbit who believes the fullness of revelation is only in his way of thinking.

The personification of the rabbit's modus operandi occurs in the area of private devotions. The rabbit believes that only those devotions and liturgical options, of which he approves, have a place in the faith life of the parish community; devotions (rosary, charismatic prayer group, and novenas) contrary to theirs thus have no place in the parish. The spectrum of private devotions is a wonderful aid to our own spiritual development and can get us into contact with many of the saints, Mary, the mother of Jesus, the Holy Spirit, and our own parish patron saints. In our parish the private devotion of adoration of the Blessed Sacrament has brought numerous blessings, some of which will be mentioned throughout this book. It is powerful to witness people, who are not even assigned to a particular hour, gathered in private prayer. However, a parish cannot be left to grow solely on private devotions. It must always center itself around public devotion; the prayer of the community gathered around the Table of the Word and the great gift of Eucharist, the Body and Blood of Jesus, "Which will be shed on behalf of many for the forgiveness of sins." (Mt. 26:28).

Our strengthened faith flows from communal worship; our private causes and our private devotions and/or individual issues supplement our public worship; but never can they take precedence over the community. If the rabbit perceives that his or her private devotions are more important than the community gathered around the Table of the Lord, it is very possible that the cycle of parish hopping will once again occur.

Occasionally, a person has asked after a weekend liturgy, "Father, can't you do anything about the people who stand around after mass and talk; I want to say my prayers and get distracted with their chatter!" If Sunday worship is seen as a "me and God" event, then the "chatter" of others becomes a distraction. When Sunday worship is understood as a communal celebration of praise and thanksgiving to God, "chatter," conversation, and fellowship are natural results. When one fully understands the public celebration of the mass there is never a desire to follow such a celebration with a private devotion. Public worship calls for a public communal response.

Every parish needs a variety of private devotions: prayer groups, intercessory prayer groups, daily rosary, private adoration of the Blessed Sacrament, charismatic prayer groups, avilas (groups who pray for vocations) and other private devotions. One private devotion that I believe should be fostered in each parish is one to its patron saint. I have read a great deal about Saint John Neumann and have encouraged parishioners to do the same. While visiting the crypt and shrine of Saint John Neumann in Philadelphia, I came across a nine-day novena to him and have given it to many people. As a parish, we believe his intercession has brought many miracles to numerous people within and outside of our parish. At least four healings of cancer have been reported to us as a result of Saint John Neumann's intercession; testimony of doctors affirms these healings.

No matter how strong my private devotions, they must never take precedence over communal prayer and liturgical worship. It is easy to think that what I feel is necessary for salvation is what the parish should center itself around; but the fullness of revelation was never revealed just to me or any one person.

There's a story about a young man who went to a guru and asked about Sunday mass. "I can worship God just as well in the woods, reading the Bible or simply by myself at home," he said. The guru happened to be at a fireplace and simply took thongs to pull out a piece of charcoal. He held it in front of the young man's face and let him watch it burn out. Then he put it back into the fire with the other pieces of charcoal. The piece that had burned out was set ablaze and burning once again. The man simply said, "Now, I understand."

If we live only with our way of thinking, focusing on our private devotions, it is possible we, too, will burn out as we will always be hopping from one place to another, seeking out people and communities who support our beliefs. But if we unite and reunite ourselves with the Body of Christ, the power of God can begin to transform our lives. Just as a piece of charcoal fizzles out by itself so, too, will we if we are of the opinion that our beliefs take precedence over the community of God's people. What we believe as essential to our salvation must be placed within the entire tradition and teachings of the church.

All of us have been told by our mothers that carrots are good for our eyesight. My nephew Brian, an avid outdoorsman, tells me rabbits have excellent eyesight. I guess that's where the old "eat your carrots" comes from; rabbits eat a lot of them. We need to have the vision of seeing the fullness of God revealed in the total community: the prayer, the Word and the celebration of Eucharist. There are many wonderful devotions, which enhance our spirituality: however, without rootedness in liturgical worship, we will never see or be the entire Body of Christ. As we plug ourselves more into the Faith Community (The Body of Christ present today) we will see how we can: (1) bring compassion to the suffering; (2) mourn with those who mourn, and laugh with those who laugh; (3) reach out to those who are hurting or allow another to touch us when we need to be touched, embraced or ministered to; (4) truly pray with another and allow another to pray with us; (5) see how God has blest us with so much and thus we can reach out to those less fortunate and lend a hand to the needy, the homeless. In short, we will understand how my private prayer and devotions flow from the entire Body of Christ gathered around the Table of the Lord and how the prayer of that assembled community can strengthen my prayer and devotions.

The rabbit's redeeming side is that it calls us to ask if I see myself as a part of the Body of Christ and how open I am to the growth The Body of Christ offers me. In addition, they challenge me to consider if I receive Eucharist for my own spiritual growth or whether I become the Body of Christ I have consumed. Those who are hurting in the community perhaps need my time. Those who have suffered loss need understanding. Those whom I have a hard time accepting need my support. Those who have hurt me need my forgiveness as I need to ask forgiveness from those I have offended. Through my actions I become the Body of Christ I have received.

All of this is a part of the Body of Christ. Public prayer calls for a public response. As a result the reception of the Body of Christ can never become just another private devotion. To do so will only cause havoc in our own personal lives as well as the faith community. In many cases, it will only give permission for one to start parish hopping.

Recently, I heard a story that has caused a lot of reflection for me. The people whom I have shared it with have also commented that they, too, have found it very thought provoking.

It seems that a famous art collector saw his son go off to war. He had all the famous paintings of prominent artists, both past and present. During the war his son was killed and the news caused the art collector a great deal of grief. As the man approached his final years, long after his son's death, he heard a knock on the door. Upon opening the door he was surprised to see a man he had never seen in his life.

"Excuse me, sir," the man said. "I was next to your son when he was killed in the war and I drew this pencil sketch of him to give you. It is the way I remember your son but I was unable to locate you. Now that I have I want you to have the sketch."

Obviously, the man was very moved. However, a week later he died and about a month after his death a great auction was held of all his famous paintings. The first thing to be auctioned off, however, was the pencil sketch of his son.

"What do I hear for this picture?" the auctioneer asked.

"C'mon," the people countered. "Let's get on with the real paintings!"

"I'm sorry," replied the auctioneer. We cannot proceed until this sketch is sold.

After a great amount of laughter, one person said: "Alright! I'll give you ten cents for the sketch!"

"Ten cents! Going once—twice—sold!!!"

The people were now excited that they could move on with the 'real auction!' However, suddenly they heard the auctioneer say, "Thank you, ladies and gentlemen, for coming. This concludes our auction. Have a good day."

"But wait!" cried the people. "What about all those other famous paintings?"

"Oh, those," responded the auctioneer. "You see, the master left one simple instruction about the auction. Whoever buys the son gets all the rest!"

Is it not true that when we accept Jesus we have to accept the mission that He gives to us and all that that entails. The essence of any parish community will always be to bring Jesus and His teachings to one another more than what I believe is essential for the growth of the parish.

I was surprised to find out that rabbits will eat tree bark in the winter. That doesn't seem appetizing to me, but they must eat to survive. As a rabbit hops into a parish, may we find our strength in the Body and Blood of Jesus and invite the rabbit to The Supper of the Lord. Rabbits normally do not make any noise: in fact, the only time they will is when their predator is trapping them for its fur. Through our communal prayer, we pray we can free the rabbit from the greatest enemy, itself, and bring them around God's table to discover the power of Jesus working through the community.

CHAPTER 2

THE KANGAROO

"I'm sorry, you must first dial '1' and the area code of the number you are calling!"

The city of Cleveland, like many other major cities, went through a whole new area code system back in April of 1998. I felt frustrated as I tried to get used to the new system. I heard the operator's voice telling me to redial so many times I felt as if I knew her.

For the first few weeks she interrupted almost every call I made. I had to re-program my speed dial after I found the numbers of friends and family, since I was so used to just pushing a button to reach them; suddenly their numbers had to be re-entered with new area codes. Frustration! Frustration! Frustration!

One of the frustrating themes of our spirituality is the need to "Let go, let God!" It is very frustrating, since we know how much we desire to control our lives. I have always said if God ever resigns from being in charge of the universe, I'll be glad to step in and take over and show how things should be. And I suspect many others would also apply for that position.

As often as I try to give all to the Lord, there are many times I hold back. Over the last couple of months I have shared with parishioners, on two or three occasions, how I always end my prayer when I pray the Divine Office, or the rosary, or when I spend time before the Blessed Sacrament. Basically, I always ask for the gift of abandonment to God's Divine Plan. And yet I know, there are many times, I probably don't even mean it. In fact, on numerous occasions I honestly hope God hasn't heard me because it's scary to say those words. While the end result of abandoning ourselves to God is always peaceful and fulfilling, it is frustrating to, "Let go and let God!"

Those words, "Let go and let God" are what I would associate with the kangaroo. It is an animal of our zoo that tells us a lot about letting go to God, since a mother kangaroo will protect her new-born in its pouch for nearly a year. They gradually release their babies and wean them to a point where they can live an independent existence. At times, however, they do allow them back into their pouch, even though there is a slow but steady releasing of their offspring.

That concept, the fact of the mother kangaroo preparing her offspring for life, staying with it and finally releasing it brings the kangaroo into our zoo. Because of this she is able to enrich the life of the baby kangaroo with the proper nurturing in the pouch. While kangaroos are capable of destroying property and gardens when they are hungry, the greater damage would be for the mother to keep her offspring too long within her pouch.

Within the parish setting, and really within society, it is the call of parents to give their children an appropriate upbringing and then step aside so the child can live God's calling in their life. Some kangaroos take up to a year to release their young. Unfortunately, it can go on much longer in the lives of some at the parish level. When this happens it can be unhealthy and counter-productive, especially if the kangaroo makes decisions for an adult child and tries to overprotect him or her from facing the realities and responsibilities of their own faith-commitment. In so doing they are hindering and destroying the possibility of personal growth in one's relationship with God.

When a kangaroo in the parish holds on to its young too long, there can be a great deal of frustration, both for the parent, the child and the minister working with them. The frustration arises because it's a no-win situation. No matter what decision is made you somehow never satisfy the baby kangaroo or the parent kangaroo.

"Father, my daughter doesn't go to church and wants her baby baptized. Would you do it?" The kangaroo, whose daughter does not go to church, wants the baby baptized, as any grandmother would. However, she does not allow her daughter to call the church. And in keeping the baby kangaroo in the pouch, frustration starts. Despite the fact the daughter needs to take responsibility for her own faith commitment, the mother wants to do what she feels is best for the daughter and grandchild.

In the above situation one could make a case for saying that the baby should not be baptized by asking who is going to give the example of practicing the faith to the child. Another side would point out the fact that you are punishing the child because of the parents. A whole topic on the theology of baptism would be necessary here, but let's just take the case as it is.

Many ministers, in attempting to reach out to the child, will ask him or her to come in for an appointment to talk about their situation and faith commitment. Most baby kangaroos will accept the invitation and, by doing so, God's graces can begin to work. However, since the son or daughter has been away from the church, they may decide, either because of fear, anger, apathy or whatever, not to come in. And in making that decision, they choose to pass up an opportunity to get their baby baptized. Unfortunately, the kangaroo parent and child, who has been away from the church, perceive the attempt at reaching out as a sign the child cannot be baptized. And the frustration level rises. "Let go and Let God!"

Whenever the baby kangaroo approaches me outside the protective pouch, I, and many ministers, welcome discussions and conversations with people in the above example. It is a wonderful time to allow the power of God to evangelize. It is a great opportunity to dialogue with the parties involved to see if a hurt in their past has taken them away from the church. If so, is it time to "Let go and let God" and move on with life? What good will it ever do a person to allow a human being in the church, no matter what role they may have had, or what hurt they may have inflicted, to have determined his or her commitment to God?

In describing some of the tendencies of the kangaroo, we mentioned, earlier on, that the mother kangaroo will often take the baby back inside her pouch. While the parent has good intentions, discussing the situation of the adult child in the presence of the over-protective parent kangaroo will be counter-productive. A face to face encounter of the minister and baby kangaroo, outside the pouch, is always more beneficial for the son or daughter to come to terms with their own attitudes and experiences of church.

Perhaps the baby kangaroo has just grown lax. Some of them will say they grew up Catholic, went to church because it was expected of them, and, when they went to college, just "got away from church." In some cases, healing often comes about as they begin talking about their lack of participation within the faith community. Many will come to understand it is now time for a new relationship with God to begin. However, some will still take the outreach of the minister as a sign Father Tim or Sister Jeanette will not allow the baby to be baptized, frustrating themselves and the minister.

Probably no situation causes more pain for a parent than to see their offspring not attending church, after raising them in a

Catholic background and bringing them up to attend mass every Sunday. Some children feel it's time to do their thing; some rebel; others join another religion; and still others are just confused. Parents need to be reassured they did not fail, and, to drop any guilt they have for their child breaking away from the church. They have done what they know is best for their child, in terms of bringing the child up with God and the church's values. If parents have provided strong roots, my experience is the child will often come back to the faith. Sometimes it can be when the fallen away Catholic's child is to be baptized or enters kindergarten. Or it may be when the child is enrolled in PSR classes for First Communion. Parents, whose children do not actively participate in the church, can be consoled that the child is God's child more than their child; and secondly, as God's child, they should never forget the tremendous power of prayer, especially to Mary, the mother of Jesus, who gave her son totally to God's will. Another model of faith is St. Monica, whose prayers were answered regarding her wayward son, St. Augustine.

Just as dealing with a kangaroo, who has been kept in the pouch too long causes frustration, so, too, many mixed feelings are generated when one releases the baby from the pouch too early.

Every summer the Strongsville Chamber of Commerce celebrates its 'home days' with a four-day festival. I have been actively involved with our city chamber at their meetings, served on a couple of city committees, and during the fall and Lenten seasons celebrate Mass with the business community at St. John Neumann Church. Because of this involvement, and being a member of the chamber, I feel it is important to help out at the festival. Have you heard the old story that you can tell a Catholic Church by the bingo sign in front of it? So it is only appropriate that I, as a Catholic priest, work at (you guessed it) the instant bingo booth.

I share this annual summer experience because it will help bring out how a kangaroo can shirk its responsibility of nurturing its young and eject the baby kangaroo, too early, from its pouch. In working the 'home days,' I always feel a sense of frustration when I sell the tickets to young children. I want to help the city, and the chamber out, but feel guilty as the children buy a ticket. I often tell them: "My father always told me you'll never get ahead trying to win money on games of chance!" And if they win a dollar, or something, I tell them to take their money and run home with it. They will never get ahead gambling on winning more.

While many parents are with their children and allow them to open their tickets and partake of their fun, there are, on the other hand, some little ones there simply by themselves. Allowing a child out of the pouch too early can easily lead a child, of grade school age, to become involved with things that simply are not healthy. When one permits the baby to wander, when it should still be inside the pouch, strange things happen. In January of 1999, two children, whose parents were not present when they were watching television, were reported to molest their half-sister after seeing it talked about on an afternoon talk show.

Before moving on to see how the kangaroo syndrome can affect all of us, there is one more area where the frustration of dealing with a kangaroo can emerge within parish ministry. And that is in the wedding preparations of the adult child. Just as we asked whether the baby should be baptized when the parents are not attending mass, so, too, we can raise the situation of two people, neither of whom attends mass, approaching the minister to be married in the church. When talking over some of the questions mentioned in our baptismal discussion, or, asking what led to their falling away from the church, various responses can be heard. Once again, praise God, a process of evangelization and healing can begin.

At times, however, some will say they are having a church wedding just to please their parents. Frustration! Frustration! Frustration! "Let go and let God." Often, after discussing Eucharist, community and the commitment of the Sacrament, ministers will request the couple to discuss and pray about what was shared during the conference in the office. The two hurry home and share what we discussed with the parent kangaroo; within a day, the parent will call and ask the minister why he is not going to marry their child in the church. As much as the parent kangaroo is assured the discussion only centered on what God is truly calling the couple to, the kangaroo is determined to jump to the conclusion that the church will not marry their daughter. Frustration! Frustration! Frustration! Let go and let God!"

While there is frustration and intense emotional levels in these situations, I have found much can be alleviated by trying to help the overly protective kangaroo realize the only person I, or any minister, should be talking to in these areas is their fully grown offspring. Often the parent kangaroo will find this difficult to accept but sooner or later it has to let the baby kangaroo out of its pouch. A minister is hindering the growth of both the parent kangaroo, and the baby kangaroo, if he or she allows the parent's desires to control the course of action.

It is also noteworthy to mention that the kangaroo can touch those who have already committed themselves to the sacrament of marriage. Many ministers have heard a couple say: "Our marriage just isn't going anywhere." Or, "We've just never grown together!" However, many opportunities simply passed both by where God could have been a part of the marriage. Praying together, being a part of each other's joys and sorrows, successes and failures, hopes and dreams; also, many times God's forgiveness could have been shared. But somehow, someway, the couple stayed inside the pouch of the kangaroo in the world, a world which always seems to tell us there is something more important than God. Rather than having twenty years of marital growth together with God and His community, the reality is one year of experience done twenty times.

The story is told of a man who spent a week's vacation at a resort and every night went to the concert on the beach given by the local community band. The conductor noticed his presence every evening, and, after the week's entertainment went up to the man and thanked him for coming. The man simply responded: "I hate to tell you this, I didn't enjoy the music at all but this was the last place my wife would look for me!"

We need to be honest and say that many of us, as we grew up, often attended mass and Eucharist because our parents made us do it. Thank God we had these values instilled into us. The truth were known there were probably times in our life that we, like the man at the concert, did not enjoy going and we were just "there." That's okay! But sooner or later we have to take ownership of our own faith journey and be able to look every priest, religious, parent, grandparent and parishioner in the eye and say: "I believe in Jesus as my Lord and Savior, and I believe, not because I want to please you, or because of what you told me, but because I have discovered Jesus is Lord.

Despite the frustration that arises with an over-protective kangaroo parent, I believe every priest, religious, deacon and pastoral minister is challenged to bring people to those words.

The examples of baptism and wedding hopefully bring out the dynamics of kangaroo characteristics. But in the end, those characteristics are in all of us. The kangaroo challenges each and every member of the Eucharistic Assembly to examine their level of participation in personal and communal prayer.

As an example, it is easy for us to still be in the pouch and think that our role as a Christian and Catholic is simply fulfilled by mass on the weekend because that's what "Good Catholics" do. In doing so, however, we may impede our own personal growth. "Putting in time" could easily close our ears and hearts to a Gospel message, as illustrated in John 13. Here, Jesus washes the feet of His disciples and ministers to them. We are all prone to drift off during the reading of God's word, myself included. The realization, as that beautiful passage brings out, that there are times in our lives we need others to minister to us is missed because we were still in the pouch of obligation. Frustration often again arises. In short, staying in the pouch by just "fulfilling our obligation" can be self-centered and self-glorifying. One can even attend mass to make themselves feel good. And yet Jesus never came to make us 'feel good' but to elevate us to His Father's Kingdom. The purpose of parish communities being centered around the Eucharist, in prayer, is not for our own good but to bring the peace and healing of Jesus to one another and to teach us how to live with The Father, The Son and The Holy Spirit.

During my high school and college days of the sixties, the Cathedral of St. John's had a 2:00am mass on Sunday morning. It was often call the printer's mass, and many would attend it to 'get mass over with!' In those days we were still living on the assumption that if you got to mass before the priest took the veil off the chalice you attended mass because you were there for, at that time, the three principal parts of the mass, i.e., the offertory, the consecration and the priest's communion.

Such experiences caused us to miss the life-giving Word of God because we were centered on ourselves. And, sad to say, I, at times, walked in "just in time!" We put in what we needed to and we were safe for another week. How can a Eucharistic Assembly grow with that kind of thinking? Can it ever be nourishing if its members are just going to "put in time?"

Some kangaroos have never matured or been allowed to mature. How can they give to the community by their regular presence and participation, at Sunday Eucharist, if they have not learned how to receive. One person in particular stands out in my memory.

Our 5:00 p.m. Christmas Eve Liturgy at St. John's is, undoubtedly, similar to any other parish Christmas Eve Liturgy. The parking lot is crowded, cars are parked everywhere, people are standing all around and pardon the phrase, "it can be a zoo!" On one occasion, while preparing for this particular mass and greeting the people, a person came up and said, "Hi, Father, good to see you. I haven't seen you since Easter!"

At first, a feeling of judgment came over me. But, after a minute or so, a feeling of sadness. Sadness because this person would not have been present if he did not have the gift of faith. He believed! Because he was there God touched his life. Just think, how much the community was missing because this person's prayer and faith were not present each Sunday. In addition, because of his absence, he was not a part of the prayer and healing of the people gathered around the Table of the Lord. He had much to offer us and the community had many blessings to share with him.

Perhaps we all can help the pouched kangaroo. If they are staying in the pouch because of a hurt in the church, a simple statement that we believe in reconciliation, in addition to inviting them to experience healing, will certainly assist one to move out of the pouch to a deeper faith commitment with Jesus and the community. Judging and condemning the baby kangaroo, because we go to church regularly and follow the commandments of our religion, will do nothing to help him or her feel a part of the community.

While frustration can set in when ministers deal with the overly protective kangaroo, or with one who releases their children too early, it is very easy to relate to them. At times, in my ministry, I have found myself leaving an assignment and still thinking about the securities I had with relationships at the former parish. It is very tempting to go through a transitional time holding on to what was, rather than to put oneself into the new community and its needs. It is easy to say "Let go and let God" but we, too, as ministers, experience the kangaroo.

In addition, I experience and have experienced the kangaroo in my own personal life. I hate to see my four-year-old great niece, Haley, growing older. The great times we have together will soon be taking on a different dimension. Change happens: it is difficult to let a parent go to God, in death, as was my experience with my father in 1987; as ministers, we, too, struggle with seeing parents growing older. Change happens: "Let go and let God!" Undoubtedly, parents struggle with letting their children go to kindergarten, graduating from grade school; and attending commencement exercises, at the high school level, certainly brings tears to the eyes and many memories to mind. Change continues: Giving one's child to marriage also provides a time of great challenge to "Let go and let God." It is a constant struggle; yet the assurance we have is that God will be with us and He will not abandon us. The words of St. Paul in his letter to the Philippians can be assuring to us:

> "...since I have indeed been taken possession of by Christ [Jesus]...forgetting what lies behind but straining forward to what lies ahead, I continue my pursuit toward the goal, the prize of God's upward calling, in Christ Jesus." (Phil. 3:12b, 13b-14)

Besides this, we have the promise and consoling words of Jesus:

"The eleven disciples went to Galilee, to the mountain to which Jesus had ordered them. When they saw him, they worshipped, but they doubted. Then Jesus approached and said to them, 'All power in heaven and on earth has been given to me. Go, therefore, and make disciples of all nations, baptizing them in the name of the Father, and of the Son, and of the holy Spirit, teaching them to observe all that I have commanded you. And behold, I am with you always, until the end of the age.' " (Mt. 28:16-20)

The ways one can stay in the pouch of the kangaroo are many, one of which is in our own prayer life. Prayer is meant to lead us to the presence of God, to let go to God, to discover that He does not abandon us, and is with us always, in all ways through each and every situation of our lives. I, like many, have felt abandonment when loved ones passed away, when tensions and anxieties existed or things simply didn't make sense. I firmly believe, however, that prayer during these moments is when God speaks to us the most.

However, if we are in the pouch and see prayer as a time to feel good, to think that whistles and bells should go off, that some tremendous emotional experience should come about, or even worse, if we grade our prayer, then staying in that pouch is truly going to do more harm than good! What will become of our faith journey with God? Ultimately, we're kidding ourselves and cheating the community. Prayer is not for our gratification but for the glory of God, to come to know God and to be assured of His faithfulness in never abandoning us. What is needed is time to pray, time to listen, time to reflect, time to say thanks, time to adore, time to just be present to Jesus. Because we live in a world of "instant everything," we cannot lay that way of life on God. Developing a relationship with Him in prayer will take time and effort. However, it is well worth it since it is so essential for our own growth, as well as that of the community.

A golfer came up to a water hole and pulled out an old ball and teed it up. Suddenly a voice came and said, "Use a new ball!" So he pulled out a new ball and took a practice swing. And once again a voice was heard to have said, "Use the old ball!"

Just as the golfer was afraid to take the risk of hitting a new ball over a water hole and wanted to stay in the pouch and use an older one, so too, we can stay in the pouch and continue doing all the "right things" about being a Catholic. God always calls us to a deeper and more meaningful relationship with Him. When He does, we should not be afraid to tee up the new ball. We can choose to stay where it is more comfortable, namely, in our own little secure prayer life, and our own private world, of what we think being a Catholic and being church should be. Or we can make a decision to take the risk of admitting our needs; that at times we are hurting and need the community's ministry to us. But, rather than venture out into unknown water, we can stay in our own little comfort zone. Similarly, we can begin thanking God daily for our blessings and realize the ministry that is ours to share. While we may feel uncomfortable going to where we have never traveled before, and feel like a voice is telling us to go back to the old ball, God loves us too much to allow us to remain only where we are comfortable. In fact, if we have a feeling of comfort, we can rest assured God is calling us out of it. All of us, as a children of God, have been blest with many gifts and talents. Jesus simply asks us to share those with one another to bring about His Father's Kingdom.

A kangaroo defends itself by kicking its feet. If we find ourselves resisting God's call to us, it may be that the kicking of our feet is why we experience frustration in our lives. Sharing our blessings with others, especially the oppressed, the needy, and the

CHAPTER 3

THE DOG

In the homes of many families there has always been room for one more member within the walls of the house, namely, the family dog. When I was in the second grade, I remember, very vividly, my mom and dad getting one of the litter from some good friends of theirs for my sister and me; "Bobo" suddenly was the fifth member of our family.

For ten years, almost until the time I graduated from high school, Bobo was a part of my daily life. We spent a lot of time together; playing in the backyard, running around at picnics, walking after school to take care of her needs, and watching television together. During my senior year, when we had to put Bobo to sleep, there were the usual tears and pains of separation that a boy has with his dog.

Undoubtedly, we have all heard the saying that a dog is "man's best friend," and, having lived with Bobo for ten years, it is easy to see how those words came about. However, as we all know, a dog can be very demanding of the time and attention of the master and often an excess amount of energy needs to be given to it. There were many times when I didn't feel like expending that energy and I would remind my sister that Bobo was just as much her dog as mine. While being "man's best friend," the dog can also wear you out.

Such is the scenario in parish ministry when a person with canine characteristics comes into the life of a minister. As a dog has his master, so too, a dog in parish life, adopts a person as "his minister." Because one is "their minister," the dog feels that he or she should always be there when the dog desires "their minister's" attention.

I remember how Bobo would need care when I came home from school. She had needs to be met, and if I would ignore her, she would let me know. After jumping on me she would run to the door, then back to me, back to the door until I finally would say; "Ok! Just a minute. Settle down!"

People are no different than that incident with Bobo. We all desire to have our needs met and look for people to meet them. But just as Bobo would hound me until I gave in, so too, dogs in the parish can feel their needs are the most important in the life of "their minister." Although Bobo obviously never knew I was away at school or playing baseball in the summertime, dogs in the life of a parish would be just the opposite as they would like to know where "their minister" is at all times.

The fact that the dog can be the farthest thing from being one's best friend in ministry is also true in everyday life, as the following two examples illustrate.

I remember a parishioner telling me how his German Shepherd was just the best dog in the world and would play with visitors and everyone in his family. However, as his daughter grew older, the Shepherd turned and attacked her. For some reason the girl was different to the dog.

On another occasion, I recall taking Communion to a woman sitting on her front porch. Her Doberman was tied up in the garage. As I pulled into the driveway, the dog started to go crazy and bark loudly at me. I told the woman, that if she wanted Communion, she'd have to pull down the garage door in order to keep the Doberman from breaking his chain and attacking. Even though there is the saying of a dog being one's best friend, I don't think I could have said that if the Doberman had jumped on me.

While it can appear I am describing a person who hinders the growth of a minister, and other parish leaders, the opposite is the case, as we shall see later on in this chapter. In describing the traits of the dog, however, it is merely my intention to bring out the point that there can be danger signs when one attempts to minister to the dog. Before painting some other characteristics, I'll share another incident from my ministry that helps us understand the dog. Although the following example involves a person whose qualities I would not liken to a dog, it will bring about the point that I am trying to make. In fact, the person, whom we will call Betty, was very much trying to grow with the Lord.

Betty was a woman who belonged to a parish to which I had been previously assigned. I was surprised when Betty called just prior to Advent at my new assignment. She wanted to know when we would have our Advent Penance Service. When I expressed my wonderment about that, she mentioned she and her family always enjoyed coming to confession to me and thus wanted to come during Advent. My response to her was, "Betty, I haven't done my job as a priest. I've gotten you more in touch with my spirit of sharing reconciliation than with the healing, forgiving power of God in the sacrament." Betty, who did have a deep love for God's forgiveness, stated that she would think over what I had said, and, during the following week, called back and said they would be going to confession in the church where I had previously been.

I want to again emphasize that the above is an illustration of a person I believe would not necessarily fit the initial description of the dog that has been mentioned. In contrast to Betty, the dog in parish life is a definite challenge to any minister.

After Bobo took up residence in our house, there was a time for the two of us to get to know each other, as well as Bobo getting acquainted with my parents and sister. My parents set up some boundaries within our home as to where Bobo could and could not go. Initially, Bobo tested us all by crossing these lines. While we will discuss the boundaries later, suffice it to say here that the initial month or so saw all of us getting to know one another.

Similarly, within the context of parish ministry, people who desire to have "their minister", have a period where they, too, try to get to know the minister. At the parish celebration of Eucharist on Sunday, they "just happen" to always be present at your Mass, and if Sister or Father starts a new group they volunteer to help. As the period of getting to know the minister continues, dogs can find themselves hanging around after a meeting to ask questions, and, in the process, share some of the issues of their life. And even though they are just in the initial phases of any kind of relationship with the minister, they feel that if they do have a problem, the minister, to whom they have attached themselves, is the only one who can solve it.

In an extreme form dogs may even develop fantasies about "their minister," "their priest," "their religious," "their friend!" As a result, they take delight in other parishioners knowing they have a special relationship with Father, Sister, the parish council president or whomever.

A few other traits of the dog deserve mentioning, one of which derives from the earlier example of the German Shepherd turning on the girl.

When I heard the story about the German Shepherd, I wondered why. Why, when one had spent so many years with that particular animal, would he turn against her? I suppose I'll never know but I wonder if it could have been that as she grew older, there were suddenly other interests and situations that were demanding more and more of her time, and, as a result, less and less attention was given the dog. Some dogs become possessive, and if you talk to others too long or spend too much time with them, they can turn on you. An associate of mine actually tells me that she was once talking to the owner of a Doberman when suddenly the Doberman attacked her and caused bleeding in her leg.

In parish ministry, since the Father or Sister is "their minister," the dog, likewise, can turn on them because the minister is spending too much time with another person or an organization. Or it may simply be that their presence was not acknowledged because they failed to receive the greeting they believed they should have gotten from their "master," who, in their life, has become "their minister." While I fail to understand totally why the shepherd pounced on that particular girl, it only stands to reason why dogs turn on "their minister." When people see another as their personal savior and feel ignored, it is only natural for them to take out their frustration. They have reached a point where the minister is perceived as "their master" and assume the minister needs the dog.

How many people in our world are searching, looking or desiring someone to come into their life and fulfill all of their needs? How many lonely people spend evenings at adult bars hoping to find the one special person, or someone who will entertain them, listen to them or just talk to them? When people are lonely or feel abandoned, it is easy to turn to drugs, sex, over-eating or alcohol as the cure. Others will turn to work or unfaithful relationships. In extreme forms, others may even turn to suicide. They think their needs will be met by one of the above remedies. And yet, as ministers, we have to remember and trust that God is the only one who can totally fulfill our needs.

In looking to help the person with characteristics of a dog, it is certainly important to get them in contact with the Body of Christ and the prayer of the community more than oneself. It is no secret that come March, the orange barrels, scattered over the various interstates and highways of our country, will return. Construction! Construction! Construction!

One of the scenes that always takes place during that time is when three lanes go into two or two get squeezed into one. If all cooperate, traffic moves smoothly. (OK, maybe not always!) And yet there are always those who know the closed lane is coming and drive right up to the point where merging becomes necessary. They dare you not to take care of their need which could have been avoided if proper merging had taken place.

Is that, perhaps, not similar to what happens with the dog? They want the attention of the minister, and, at times, go to great lengths to merge. But what is more essential for the minister is to get them to merge into the growth and movement of the entire community. Otherwise the minister and community can drive right by them and cause a lot of pain and hurt.

While I was preparing to leave a parish, I happened to mention to a brother priest that this assignment was good. I had learned a lot, but I was wondering about the people God had sent into my life to be touched by my ministry. They had been a part of my growth and I had been a part of theirs. What would happen to them? He said something to me I have never forgotten, "Bob, your job was not to get them in touch with you, but with God!" How true that is.

The danger for any minister, as might have been the case for me back then, is to see the dog as important to his or her ministry. Dogs are a challenge. Like the household pet that you need to spend a lot of time with, they need to be affirmed and told they are important. Because they want to spend time with you and tell you how much you are helping them solve their problems, they can make you feel good about yourself and your ministry. In reality, however, they are hurting and needy persons. Because dogs are affirmed by the minister and are being helped by him to solve all of their problems, there is a potentially dangerous situation. And this is simply that the minister begins to rely on the dog's "warm fuzzies" and he can become a dog because of mutual needs.

How true this can be even if we go back to Bobo or any household dog. Many are the times I would come home and expect Bobo to greet me. If I would be watching television in the family room downstairs, I expected her to come and watch with me. Every morning I depended on her to eat the corner of my peanut butter toast. I would throw it in the air and knew she would be there to catch it. At first I would look at her. But after a while it was just a ritual. I expected Bobo to be there.

The minister can never forget that one's source of strength and affirmation is his or her personal prayer life with God, Jesus and The Spirit. Because we all have needs, it is easy to see how one can become a dog as a minister of the church. If that happens and we allow the dog to prevail, not only will the minister suffer, but we will be stunting the dog's personal, psychological, emotional and spiritual growth as well as hurting the growth of the entire Body of Christ.

It is only natural for the minister to try to understand the dog. What kind of relationship is missing in dogs' lives as they use any means available to manipulate the minister to fulfill their needs, whatever they may be? The bottom line is no human being can fulfill the total needs of another; no creature can bring to another the total fulfillment and intimacy one desires. Only God Himself can. How did St. Augustine say it? "Our hearts are restless until they rest in Thee!" And perhaps our ministry is simply to get them in touch with the loving, forgiving, healing God of their life more than ourselves. It takes a wise and healthy minister to know the fine line between helping and enabling.

A young man wanted to join a monastery and went to the guru to ask him if he knew the perfect monastery. The guru said he had found one many years ago but chose not to enter. When asked why he did not, the guru simply answered, "If I had joined, it would no longer have been perfect!"

We are all very fragile people with imperfections, needs and desires. No one person can ever be the one who takes care of all of what is needed in our life. We are not members of the Body of Christ because we are perfect but imperfect. That is why Jesus gave His life for us. And that death and resurrection of Jesus, as experienced by the motley crew within the community, is what the dog must experience. In the end, only Jesus can bring the necessary healing.

Besides the minister pointing to God, Jesus, The Spirit and the Body of Christ, two other points are essential. One involves boundaries, and another, a sidetrack on the sacrament of reconciliation.

Earlier in this chapter I mentioned that my parents did a wonderful job of training Bobo, regarding where she was allowed to be in our home, and where she was not. She could watch television with us in the downstairs family room and be in the kitchen; but the living room and dining room were out of bounds. They set up appropriate boundaries for Bobo.

In dealing with dogs, boundaries are essential because what is needed in the dog's life is contact, not with the minister, but with God's healing power. They need to be the best friend of a forgiving, loving and healing God. Only when they do that and solve their own problems can the minister and the community be of any help to them. The minister takes responsibility for setting healthy boundaries so that others can learn independence and growth. Often, it is a case where the person looks to the minister to provide emotional support because of abuse, abandonment or deprivations in his life. Through appropriate boundaries, the minister leads the person into contact with his or her feelings about relationships that have been lacking. True healing can now begin. Only then can the dog and minister live and work in a healthy balance.

Secondly, in regard to helping the dog, permit me, if you will, a little excursus regarding the sacrament of reconciliation. There is probably no sacrament more misunderstood in our church than that of confession. Even the word confession sounds a little "yucky" as we confess to a judge, a police officer or to whomever we are forced to confess our guilt. So many people believe this sacrament is a ticket or permission slip to go to communion and miss the fact that it is a personal encounter with the forgiveness and healing power of God. As long as confession is just getting permission to go to communion, it will never mean anything. This kind of thinking can often stem from the belief that one has to earn God's reconciliation or somehow twist God's arm to forgive. God's love and forgiveness is a free gift and one never has to buy it or do certain things to merit it. We cannot make God love us more than He already does. If one is of the mindset that they have to "jump through hoops" to earn God's forgiveness, it will be difficult to see God as one's friend and confession will be viewed simply as a "thing" to do. However, wrestling and reflecting on God's forgiveness through Jesus will only cause growth in one's relationship with God.

Dogs desire permission to be a best friend and crave for a sign of approval to know they still have a relationship. Similar to one who feels he has to earn God's forgiveness in reconciliation, the dog, too, will seek to earn the minister's approval. However, to help them get a better awareness and to avoid game playing, it is essential they come to encounter the forgiveness, love and healing power of God. In the sacramental form of forgiveness, the priest minister, who is the dog's "special minister," may or may not be the best one to help accomplish forgiveness, love and healing. However, another pastoral minister, spiritual director, mentor or professional counselor can certainly guide them into the proper healing of past relationships and start the process of healing and pointing them in the direction of God.

The relationship of those who are dogs and "their minister" can be deadly for both, especially when the ministers do not clarify their roles, namely, one who points to God. Otherwise we can encounter Chapter 32 of the Book of Exodus coming alive.

> "When the people became aware of Moses' delay in coming down from the mountain, they gathered around Aaron and said to him, 'Come, make us a god who will be our leader; as for the man Moses who brought us out of the land of Egypt, we do not know what has happened to him.' Aaron replied, 'Have your wives and sons and daughters take off

the golden earrings they are wearing, and bring them to me.' So all the people took off their earrings and brought them to Aaron who accepted their offering, and fashioning this gold with a graving tool, made a molten calf. Then they cried out, 'This is your God, O Israel, who brought you out of the land of Egypt. On seeing this, Aaron built an altar before the calf and proclaimed, 'Tomorrow is a feast of the Lord.' Early the next day the people offered holocausts and brought peace offerings. Then they sat down to eat and drink, and rose up to revel.

With that, the Lord said to Moses, 'Go down at once to your people, whom you brought out of the land of Egypt, for they have become depraved. They have soon turned aside from the way I pointed out to them, making for themselves a molten calf and worshipping it, sacrificing to it and crying out, 'This is your God, O Israel, who brought you out of the land of Egypt!'" (Ex. 32:1-8)

Dogs remind us we can easily go barking up the wrong tree and play games within ourselves when we believe another is our personal savior rather than The Lord. As we have already mentioned, no one person, absolutely no one, no priest, religious, lay person, no institution, nothing, nothing, nothing can bring us fulfillment and ultimate happiness and peace except God.

Dogs challenge us to find the source of our identity:
- Is it in other people?
- Is it what other people are saying about us?
- Is it how many people affirm us?
- Is it in how much wealth or possessions I accumulate?

Ultimately, everything will pass away; but the love, forgiveness and healing touch of God will remain with us always into the great gift of eternal life.

Recently on my day off I was sitting at the table with my mother; to my surprise she told me that she often looks out the window at the birds and thinks of the scripture passage where God takes care of them. Perhaps that teaching of Jesus from Matthew is something not only the dog, but the minister, also, must keep in mind as God does, and will, provide for our needs.

> "Therefore I tell you, do not worry about your life, what you will eat or drink, or about your body, what you will wear. Is not life more than food and the body more than clothing? Look at the birds in the sky; they do not sow or reap, they gather nothing into barns, yet your heavenly Father feeds them. Are not you more important than they? Can any of you by worrying add a single moment to your life span? Why are you anxious about clothes? Learn from the way the wild flowers grow. They do not work or spin. But I tell you that not even Solomon in his entire splendor was clothed like one of them. If God so clothes the grass of the field, which grows today and is thrown into the oven tomorrow, will he not much more provide for you, O you of little faith?... Seek first the kingdom [of God] and his righteousness" (Mt. 6:25-30, 33).

It is here, perhaps, we find our identity: when we take a leap of faith and seek first God's Kingdom, He provides for all of our needs

Like some of the other animals in the zoo, it is important to have people in the parish with characteristics of a dog as they can assist the community in its growth. They allow us to stay in contact with the fact that it is God who ultimately touches people. It is He who saves, He who died for our sins and not we!

Finally, we should be thankful to the dogs because they lead us to honesty, an honesty which leads to truthfulness about ourselves and authenticity in our prayer. Our prayer, in dealing with dogs, should not only be to become a true instrument of God, but for the dogs to get the help they need which often can only be provided by a professional counselor or therapist.

Not only the prayer of the minister can assist the dogs but also that of the community. If a parish really begins meetings with prayer, faith-sharing, scripture (especially the scriptures from the upcoming Sunday), petitions, a blessing of parishioners, the invocation of the Holy Spirit for guidance and direction, then parishioners, and especially the dogs, have instilled in them a realization that God is their pastor, God is our savior, God is our healer, and that God is the person who gave us Jesus out of His love to bring forgiveness and the Kingdom of God to us.

This is so important in parish life since dogs can, in addition to their relationship with "their minister," hook onto an organization, or a renewal program, and suddenly this is the beginning and the end of their life. Again, no program or organization will be the savior of people. In my ministry I have seen various programs come and go. It only teaches us that God and His salvific act of Redemption is what will save us.

Perhaps Henri Nouwen says it best in a book entitled: Henri Nouwen, Writings Selected With an Introduction by Robert A. Jonas, published by Orbis Books, 1998. In Nouwen's letters to Marc, we read the following:

> "The most important thing you can say about God's love is that God loves us not because of anything we've done to earn that love, but because God, in total freedom, has decided to love us. At first sight, this doesn't seem to be very inspiring, but if you reflect on it more deeply this thought can affect and

influence your life greatly. We're inclined to see our whole existence in terms of quid pro quo; you scratch my back, and I'll scratch yours. We begin by assuming that people will be nice to us if we are nice to them; they will help us if we help them; that they will invite us if we invite them; that they will love us if we love them. And so the conviction is deeply rooted in us that being loved is something you have to earn. In our pragmatic, and utilitarian times this conviction has become even stronger. We can scarcely conceive of getting something for nothing. Everything has to be worked for, even a kind word, an expression of gratitude, a sign of affection.

I think it's this mentality that lies behind a lot of anxiety, unrest and agitation... The enormous propensity to seek recognition, admiration, popularity and renown is rooted in the fear that, without all this, we are worthless. You could call it the 'commercialization' of love. Nothing for nothing. Not even love.

The result is a state of mind that makes us live as though our worth as human beings depended on the way others react to us. We allow other people to determine who we are. We think we're good if other people find us so; we think we're intelligent if others consider us intelligent; we think we're religious if others think so too... Thus, we sell our souls to the world. We're no longer master in our own house. Our friends and enemies decide who we are. We've become the playthings of their good or bad opinion...

The tragic thing, though, is that we humans aren't capable of dispelling one another's loneliness and lack of self-respect. We humans haven't the capacity to relieve one another's most radical predicament. Our ability to satisfy one another's deepest longing is so limited that time and time again we are in danger of disappointing one another...Everything that Jesus had done, said and undergone is meant to show us that the love we most long for is given to us by God, not because we've deserved it, but because God is a God of love...

If we had a firm faith in God's unconditional love for us, it would no longer be necessary to be always on the lookout for ways of being admired by people, and we would need, even less, to obtain from people by force what God desires to give us so abundantly---pp. 22-23, Letters to Marc, 49-52.

One of the first things Catholics learned was the commandments. One of them simply stated: I am the Lord thy God, thou shalt not have strange gods before me. It is truly our role and privilege to open up new ways for the dogs to "see" the one whom we all serve. He is within us and beyond us. When they touch Jesus, and are touched by Jesus, they no longer need "their minister!"

CHAPTER 4

THE RACCOON

On August 3, 1998, the city of Cleveland and its surrounding area had a terrible rain storm. Highways were flooded, floating cars were stranded in the middle of interstates, and many residents saw their basements flooded.

Strongsville, where St. John Neumann is located, was no exception. A few days after that torrential downpour, a parishioner mentioned to me after our 9:00 am mass that a fellow-parishioner was suing the city for his flooded basement. Later, after having shared this information with another parishioner, a feeling of embarrassment came over me (an embarrassment I truly deserved) because I found out that the person suing the city was not our parishioner, but only one with a similar name. Because I had failed to go to the source, I had gossiped!

In the years I have been ministering, it seems to me that an animal that can hurt people and a parish community a great deal is the raccoon. By feeding itself on the garbage of others, and by saying things that are not true, often with no basis in reality, the raccoon distracts a parish from centering itself around Eucharist and prayer. In short, the raccoon is not only destructive, but abusive as well.

The opening example brings out how rumors spread when one fails to go to the source. This behavior has no place in a parish community and only leads the community astray from its primary focus to bring the peace, healing and love of Jesus to others. The raccoon only causes havoc.

I have always been sensitive about sharing the condition of someone in the hospital when approached by a fellow-parishioner. While the inquiry is done very compassionately and with sincere concern, I learned very early that an innocent statement like, "Ron was having a little trouble breathing," can come back to you, after traveling through a number of people as, "Ron had a quadruple bypass surgery!" Not only is the family shocked when they hear this and that it came from the mouth of Father, or the pastoral minister, but I am, too. If we should always go to the source it makes more sense for us to direct questions to the family when asked how a person is doing.

Situations like the flooded basement and questions about one in the hospital help reveal the first way the gossip of a raccoon can make its presence known, and that is not going to the source. When the raccoon fails to go to the source, the garbage of others will provide much nourishment. Similar to me in the above example, raccoons gossip! Gossipers repeat the words of others who have no facts themselves because of their own failure to go to the source.

"But, Father, I know Mary and the one thing she would not do is lie to me!" Mary may not have lied but did the party go to the source?

"You don't understand, Sister, I have it from a very reliable source that the Woman's Club, the K of C, the Holy Name, the Liturgy Committee, are going to do this or that!" The group may very well have something planned; however, did the party again go to the source?

"Tom has been around here for years and if anyone would know the facts he would, Father! Trust me!" Tom probably has been a pioneer of the parish; but has the party gone to the source?

Throughout each and every day, we hear many similar statements! We have listened to them at the office, the mall, soccer games, parish meetings, family gatherings, restaurants and school functions. The one constant, however, is that in most cases people never went to the source. Very simply, when one fails to go to the source, all that is shared is gossip.

Failing to go to the source affects not only the individual but the community as well since the dignity and reputation of both can be destroyed. At its best, it lowers the sacredness of a people striving to center themselves around Eucharist and prayer; at its worst, it annihilates individual lives and the faith community.

It is said that while St. Philip Neri was hearing confessions a lady came in and confessed she had been gossiping about others. St. Philip gave her a strange penance whereby she was to take the unplucked fowl in a market place and on her way home pull out its feathers, one by one, and throw them on the street. When she finished this she was to return to him. It was a different penance but the lady did what St. Philip told her.

Upon arriving back at the church, the saint instructed her that to complete her penance she would have to go back and pick up all the feathers. The lady protested saying it was impossible since they had all been blown away by the wind and how could anyone expect to find all those feathers again! Saint Philip merely responded by telling her she was right and that, likewise, one can never get back the damaging words about one's neighbors by the time they have passed from one person to another. He then asked her to be careful in the future and to watch the words that came from her mouth.

I sometimes wonder if we ever master the urge to gossip. All too often, not only is the raccoon around the parish but, unfortunately, I find myself being a raccoon. Can it be that it is easier to point out the faults and failings of others in order to avoid confronting our own faults? This evasion brings about the second way a raccoon can strike and that is through blaming another! Rather than expose myself to God's call in my life at the present moment, it is easier to blame another, often at the expense of truth.

One does not need a degree to see that we are quickly becoming a society that believes in scapegoating. If I can put the blame on another instead of admitting my own mistakes, it is easier to control and manipulate life than to look at where God may be calling me to grow. Isn't it amazing how we, while driving, can be upset with the person in front of us for going too slow and, yet, at other times, believe the person driving behind us is in such a hurry?

Often, in parish life, an organization will have had an annual function which may have gone on for five, ten, twenty or thirty years, maybe even longer. But sooner or later, it just no longer flies. Different people have moved in, new goals take the parish in other directions and people seem less interested in what used to be the event of the parish.

It is here the raccoon's scapegoating can move in; and rather than face up to the truth, the scapegoating authorizes a "raccoon version" for the reason something did or did not happen.

- "It's the younger generation, they just don't want to get involved!"
- "If they'd make me feel welcome when I went to a meeting they'd get all the help they need!"
- "If Sally wasn't so busy she would have done a better job with the publicity. It's all her fault!"
- "And Andy, ever since he got in that prayer group, he couldn't care less!"

All of these reactions put the blame on another. And yet the truth flowing from the community prayer may be that the event is no longer relevant to the life of the parish. But better for the raccoons to scapegoat than to see where God is calling them and the parish community.

Although we have discussed aspects of the sacrament of Baptism in the chapter on the kangaroo, one phase of Baptism that often confronts one involved in pastoral ministry is the whole area of godparenting. And here again, the raccoon's scapegoating will move about if one does not hear what he or she wants to hear.

While the primary teachers of the child are the parents, the sacrament calls for godparents who provide an example of living the Catholic faith for the person they are called to sponsor. The parents have promised their sister, brother or whomever, the role of godparenting, only to find out that the perspective godparent cannot get a sponsor's certificate from their parish because they no longer attend mass, have chosen to join another religion or have not taken ownership for their faith by being confirmed.

This is always a touchy situation, as well as a potentially explosive one. Emotions run high and those strong feelings can bring forth comments similar to, "If that church had better homilies I'd be going! I bet if I was giving money to the church I'd have no problem getting a certificate."

While the question of godparents who do not practice the faith lends itself to much discussion, the point is that the raccoon, by scapegoating, will say things about a minister or the church rather than look at his or her relationship with God.

When I was discussing the raccoon with my nephew, I was surprised to find out raccoons are very clever and curious. If there is food in a jar they will somehow get to it. When one thing doesn't work, another is tried.

We, too, because of hidden agendas, grudges and hurts, can also be very innovative in avoiding personal growth. Unfortunately, that can mean putting the blame on another and talking about them more than facing reality ourselves.

When we go to the source of our lives, God, and understand He sent His Son, Jesus, for all, much healing can come. For example everything is not my spouse's fault. Perhaps I need to stop scapegoating and see that maybe, just maybe, the reason the marriage is not progressing is because of "the plank" in my own eye rather than the faults of my spouse. The work environment also improves when I understand that I, too, am prone to the same mistakes I accuse my co-worker of making.

It is said that two people signed up for a trip, each one desiring to have single occupancy. However, due to a mix-up, it was necessary for the two to share a room. After meeting each other, one eventually went down to the main desk and asked if he could check in his valuables since he was suspicious of the person he was forced to room with. "I know exactly what you're speaking about," said the receptionist. "He was just down here for the same reason!"

The ingenuity of the raccoon to scapegoat must give way to the love and forgiveness of God for any growth to occur.

A wonderful example of scapegoating in marriage became evident to me years ago when a parishioner, Jeff, told me about a gambling addiction that had afflicted him earlier in his life. Jeff was into heavy betting on football games and his wife told me that the only days you could live with him were Wednesday and Thursday. On Fridays he would start getting nervous about Saturday's college games and Sunday would see him glued to the television with NFL football, as well as Monday night. And Tuesdays would often see him mourning his losses.

Through God's help, Jeff overcame this addiction and he and his wife are now very happily married. The interesting insight Jeff demonstrates, however, is that when he was into heavy gambling, he always blamed his wife for not understanding him. He was trying to better the family through his winnings but she would just "nag" him. Only after he stopped the scapegoating and complaining about his wife could he face what God was calling him to in his life. He no longer fed himself by scapegoating on the perceived garbage of others. He had to change. Praise God he did.

The raccoon and his gossip can thus strike through: (1) failing to go to the source, and (2) putting the blame on another by scapegoating. A third way he becomes a predator is through assuming things.

A couple who had been married well over fifty years always planted a garden in the springtime. As the husband was on his deathbed he gathered his children around him and told them to make sure that every spring they help their mother plant the garden. "I want you to promise this to me," he said. "It was the one thing your mother always enjoyed doing." After his death, and after helping their mother grieve, the children approached her about planting the garden in the upcoming spring. "Oh, the garden," she stated. "I just did that to appease your father. It was the one thing I know he enjoyed doing. Myself—I couldn't care less if there was a garden or not!"

How easy to assume what one's motives are! How easy to assume motives of parishioners by the parish staff. How easy to assume motives of the parish staff by the parishioners. Whenever we assume motives, actions or thoughts, we face the possibility of becoming like the raccoon and feeding on the garbage of others.

This notion of assuming things of another was made very clear to me early in my priesthood. At my first assignment a couple called to have their marriage validated in the church. When we finished discussing that matter they proceeded to say they would like to have their baby baptized. "How wonderful," I said. "When is the baby due?" A legitimate question but a rather embarrassing answer came when the couple told me they already had the child a few months ago. All because I assumed the mother was pregnant from the way she looked. You can be sure I now word that question a lot differently.

An area in the church where raccoons have hurt others a great deal is in the area of marriage annulments. Normally I like to ask people when they petition for an annulment to tell me what they have heard about them. Inevitably the misconception always arises that if you have money you will get an annulment and if you do not you will be denied. After going through the erroneous information they have received from raccoons, plus other false apprehensions, we can begin the process in a much better state of mind because they are now hearing the truth from the source.

Can these misconceptions arise from raccoons who, in their own street talk with others, believed their assumptions were the truth? Again, the raccoon can be, and, is destructive.

One issue facing many parishes today is updating and expanding their facilities. Computer rooms, libraries in the schools and administration space are just a few challenges facing parish staffs. Our parish and interparochial school, Sts. Joseph and John, was no exception. In talking to other pastoral ministers, administrators and pastors who have initiated building fund drives, it is interesting to hear how the raccoons have invaded communities through their assumptions.

"If you don't give "x" amount of dollars your child will be asked to leave the school!" Could an assumption like this possibly be coming from unresolved anger regarding other issues in one's life? Whether it be in the parish, home, work or out on the streets, unresolved anger will often manifest itself through false assumptions. So much more is resolved and healed when we go to the source, who is not only the person involved, but God and His forgiveness.

One of the most beautiful gospel stories is in the fourth chapter of Saint John, the Woman at the Well (Jn.4:4-42). The woman first has some anger toward Jesus; but after being challenged by

Him to talk about some of her life experiences, she goes off to town to tell people she has met the Messiah.

"He [Jesus] had to pass through Samaria. So he came to a town of Samaria called Sychar, near the plot of land that Jacob had given to his son Joseph. Jacob's well was there. Jesus, tired from his journey, sat down there at the well. It was about noon.

A woman of Samaria came to draw water. Jesus said to her, 'Give me a drink' (For Jews use nothing in common with Samaritans...) The Samaritan woman said to him, 'How can you, a Jew, ask me, a Samaritan woman for a drink?'...Jesus said to her, 'Go call your husband and come back.' The woman answered and said to him, 'I do not have a husband.' Jesus answered her, 'You are right in saying 'I do not have a husband. For you have had five husbands, and the one you have now is not your husband. What you have said is true.' The woman said to him, 'Sir, I can see that you are a prophet'...The woman left her water jar and went into the town and said to the people, 'Come see a man who told me everything I have done. Could he possibly be the Messiah?' They went out of the town and came to him...Many of the Samaritans of that town began to believe in him because of the word of the woman...Many more began to believe in him because of his word, and they said to the woman, 'We no longer believe because of your word; for we have heard for ourselves, and we know that this is truly the savior of the world.'" (Jn. 4:1-7, 9, 16-19, 28-30, 39, 41-42).

In the beginning, it is fascinating to see how Jesus leads her to an understanding of who He is; at the end, it is also noteworthy to see how the people came to believe in Jesus as Savior of the world. However, none of this would have happened if Jesus had assumed things of the woman because she was a Samaritan or if the people had not come out to see the source of the woman's statements, Jesus Himself. When one does not assume things and goes to the source, Jesus can begin to touch people.

It is very easy in marriage and family life to give up because one believes his/her spouse will never change. And yet how will they know if they only assume things and do not go to the source of their motives? As the woman at the well and townspeople show us, when one does not assume things and goes to the source, God's graces can do wonders.

One of the things I find funny, as a priest, is when I'm at a restaurant, golf course or Jacobs Field and someone says to me: "What are you doing here?" I know this is a common question but it always strikes me as humorous since the question elicits an obvious answer. However, it's not the question that causes consternation, but how the raccoon can strike afterwards. A pastoral minister or religious woman has lunch with their brother or likewise a priest with his sister and suddenly the raccoon assumes sister was out with a man and father was out with a woman for lunch.

Parishioners, likewise, have endured similar raccoon remarks. In addition, today's media scrutiny into lives of public figures has caused not only paranoia but more and more judgments and assumptions. While we certainly have had our share of church and political scandals over the years, many good people serve our country, cities and church despite the comments generated by a raccoon's gossip. As we have maintained throughout this chapter, the raccoon is indeed deadly.

Finally, the raccoon can strike at parish meetings. All of us, in our individual educational endeavors, have taken tests where we wondered if we were at the right class when we see the questions asked on the exam. Similarly, one can wonder if they were at the same meeting a raccoon was at when the raccoon shares the meeting with others.

At times, a pastor, associate pastor or pastoral minister will want to move a group forward and raise questions regarding the group's activities or the mission of the parish. He or she may simply inquire how a certain activity relates to a particular part of the faith community. I remember a minister asking a group why their meetings did not begin with prayer. What came to me was, "Sister wants to turn us into holy-rollers!" Obviously what was asked and what was said by the raccoon differed greatly.

Like the zebra, which we will discuss later, the raccoon challenges us to stand for the truth and a greater appreciation of Eucharist and God's word. For rather than feeding on the gossip of others, we must move to the food of the Eucharistic Table. In this way we turn to the gentle, loving, forgiving God whose Son, Jesus, guides us in reaching the full potential of the Body of Christ. This will always be more nourishing than feeding on idle gossip.

Because we cannot control the raccoon's statements or what another says, the importance of turning to the Eucharist and The Body of Christ cannot be stressed enough. It is there, in the Body and Blood of Jesus and the prayer of the community, that one will find their strength and peace.

We often notice raccoons lying dead along the side of a road. If we do not go to the source, if we scapegoat, if we assume motives, or just plain gossip, we, too, will lead a very lifeless existence. But allowing the Body and Blood of Jesus to sustain us will lead not only to dying with Jesus but rising with Him to new life.

The patron saint of my present parish, St. John Neumann, was the fourth bishop of Philadelphia from 1852-1860. Whenever people disagreed over petty things and began blaming others, he would say something similar to: "Stop! Let's go before the Blessed Sacrament for thirty minutes and/or let's say the stations of the cross and then come back and discuss what we're saying in relation to what Jesus did for us." I can't wait someday to do that in a parish—especially when the raccoons are out scavenging!!

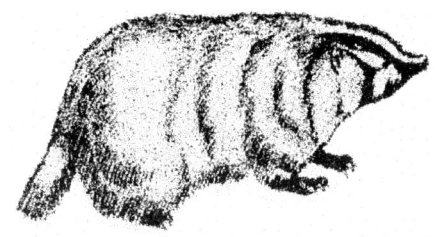

CHAPTER 5

THE BADGER

It is so easy to get caught up in ourselves, our needs, our wants, our desires that we start to develop tunnel vision. We see things through our perspective and forget the big picture. In church life it can lead to forgetting that we are part of a faith community, the faith community a part of a diocese, the diocese a part of the universal church and the universal church a part of the world.

Back in the spring of 1995 our long-range planning committee at Saint John Neumann was nearing the end of its preparation for an addition to our present church structure. As we approached the final phases of the project and moved along into the concluding stages, our architect mentioned to me that our next step would be for him and me to go downtown and meet with the Diocesan Building Commission to present our plans. When we went I was expecting him to bring in a sheet with a diagram of the building with drawings of where the corridors, foyer, activity center, restrooms, kitchen, pantry and three new meeting rooms would be located.

When I saw him come to the meeting with over 100 pages of blueprints I did a double, triple and probably even a quadruple take. "What are all those for?" I innocently asked. He then proceeded to tell me that these were the prints for the electrical wiring, the heating and air-conditioning, the lighting, the plumbing and all kinds of other things I cannot even remember. What an education I had. Did it meet city codes? Diocesan regulations? It was not just a one page drawing and certainly more than I had ever envisioned.

Just as I didn't understand everything that goes into building, similarly, we often neglect the bigger picture of God's Divine Providence. While we are quick to recognize that our needs and personal agendas should be the main focus of the church, we forget a very beautiful passage in the Gospel of Matthew.

"When the Son of Man comes in his glory, and all the angels with him, he will sit upon his glorious throne, and all the nations will be assembled before him. And he will separate them one from another, as a shepherd separates the sheep from the goats. He will place the sheep on his right and the goats on his left. Then the king will say to those on his right, 'Come, you who are blessed by my Father. Inherit the kingdom prepared for you from the foundation of the world. For I was hungry and you gave me food, I was thirsty and you gave me drink, a stranger and you welcomed me, naked and you clothed me, ill and you cared for me, in prison and you visited me.' Then the righteous will answer him and say, 'Lord, when did we see you hungry and feed you, or thirsty and give you drink? When did we see you a stranger and welcome you, or naked and clothe you? When did we see you ill or in prison, and visit you?' And the king will say to them in reply, 'Amen, I say to you, whatever you did for one of these least brothers of mine, you did for me.'

Then he will say to those on his left, 'Depart from me, you accursed, into the eternal fire prepared for the devil and his angels. For I was hungry and you gave me no food, I was thirsty and you gave me no drink, a stranger and you gave me no welcome, naked and you gave me no clothing, ill and in prison, and you did not care for me.' Then they will answer and say, 'Lord, when did we see you hungry or thirsty or a stranger or naked or ill or in prison, and not minister to your needs?' He will answer them, 'Amen, I say to you, what you did not do for one of these least ones, you did not do for me.' And these will go off to eternal punishment, but the righteous to eternal life." (Mt. 25:31-46)

There are many reflections on this passage. And while we could share various thoughts on it, we have also, and most importantly, seen many give evidence to witnessing what Jesus meant. People like the late Mother Teresa have ministered to the sick, homeless and dying. Parents in many parishes have adopted children from other environments into their homes. People throughout a diocese will spend hours feeding the hungry. Thank God followers of Jesus show us the meaning of this passage.

In contrast to this, however, the badger only sees his needs with the expectation that people will minister to them; when they do not, he has only one response—attack!

The badger makes its presence known because, like me in the building process, he lacks the total picture. This makes the badger similar to the raccoon but with these differences. While the raccoon gossips, often behind the back of another, the badger attacks the one whom he perceives as the source of his problem(s) face to face. Unlike the raccoon, the badger attacks from facts that he knows. But again, the facts lack the total picture. And finally, the raccoon will, in almost all cases, stay within the community whereas the badger will at times withdraw, and, in a small number of cases, leave. Unlike the rabbit, he moves out, (often for only a short period) not so much seeking the perfect community, but because he is upset.

One thing, however, can be said of both the raccoon and badger—they are both vicious. Even though the raccoon's gossip can hurt more people, the badger's actions are just as destructive since it is a ferocious animal and known for its tenacity. Once it starts, it will never give up. The king of the jungle, the lion, will stay away from it knowing that, if he fights with the badger, he'll have to kill it since the badger will keep coming at him. The badger never stops. You either stop it or it kills you.

And yes, there are badgers in the church!

No matter who we are we all have needs, and it is only natural to believe that people of various institutions should be there to meet them. We expect a hospital to meet our health needs, banks to sit with us and discuss our financial necessities and government officials to listen to our concerns regarding our communities. Similarly, one expects the church and its ministers to be present to their spiritual needs and growth.

The above, and many service-oriented institutions, undoubtedly do their best to be of assistance to people. There are times when they, like I, have failed. While ministers would like to meet the needs of all, there are situations when it is simply impossible.

"Sister Ann walked right by me and didn't even ask how I was doing! You think she would have taken time to at least stop and say hello!" Perhaps the attack is justified and Sister should have said hello, but on the other side of the coin, the total picture could have been that Sister had to go quickly to a home where a parishioner was seriously ill.

"Father, I was in so much pain last Wednesday when you said the morning mass. Afterwards, I really needed a hug but you went right back to the rectory!" It is obviously good for staff members to be present at Eucharistic celebrations and available after them for conversation. But again, the total picture may have been that a family was waiting in the office to make funeral arrangements.

Badgers can be anyone in a parish. Parish commissions, leaders or organizations can badger others for their time, talent and resources and try to make them feel guilty if they don't respond. As we approach the end of a millenium we are obviously in different times than we were in the early 1900's. Family life is certainly different. What might have been a viable group or organization years ago may or may not be today. And yet often a person within the church will badger one to keep the group going just to keep it going. "We have all these families and we can't get the parents to come to a meeting!" is often heard. Again, while an organization may have done much good within a parish community, its purpose for existing may no longer be a viable one because of different circumstances.

Within today's church there are many parishes who celebrate First Communion differently than thirty or forty years ago. Rather than a large group celebration, some have moved to smaller celebrations at each of the weekend parish masses. While one may disagree with the practice, the badger, if he were opposed to the change, would attack without finding out all the facts.

The administration of the Sacrament of Confirmation has also caused much consternation for the badger, especially if it has been moved into the high school level. While often there is no diocesan wide agreement as to what age this sacrament should be received, the badger springs into action if he believes Confirmation should be administered at the elementary level.

People in the business world have shared that the most difficult thing they do is to dismiss a person from their job. Often they cannot give all the facts because of confidentiality and legal issues. And because all that could be known cannot be told, the badger can again attack. I know myself that since becoming a pastor in January of 1990, I have become less critical of church decisions wider than my role as pastor. Although I still think I know better than "they" do, I realize that just as I cannot say certain things because of confidentiality, so, too, I often do not know the total picture of other institutions within our diocese or universal church.

There are times the badger's attack is justified. I know that occasionally I have failed, for one reason or another, to mention the name of the person for whom a mass is being offered at the prayer of the faithful during a weekday mass. You always feel bad when you do something like this, but grateful that most people of the family in these circumstances understand. However, there are times when the badger will attack because of this. An accusation of being insensitive or lacking in compassion would be just one of the ways he would get his teeth into you.

A popular area of the badger is church finances. Most diocesan churches present a financial homily once a year to inform parishioners how their monies are being spent. You can always spot the badger after the talk when you hear, "All the church wants is money! That's all they ever talk about!"

Family life today is often lived out in a time crunch. We are always on the move. Sometimes just having a family meal together is an accomplishment with Dad working overtime or out of town, Mom driving one kid to soccer practice and picking another up from cheerleading. And besides this, she has to get to her own parents' house to do their shopping. Because of these factors, badgers within a family can emerge. Children forget parents have feelings and that Mom and Dad face issues of aging and health problems. Parents can likewise be negligent in realizing a child is striving to find his or her own identity. Because we often take our loved ones for granted, we badger our own family members and develop a self-centered "badger mentality" all because we forget the total picture of each other's life.

Probably nothing has changed so drastically in my priesthood as hospital care and hospital visitation. As we know, people are in and out of hospitals in a manner of hours. In my first year as a priest, a hernia surgery would keep a person in the hospital for seven to ten days. Now they are home in a matter of hours. If the relative of a badger is in the hospital, the badger can jump into action the following weekend at the celebration of Eucharist. "You never went to visit my husband in the hospital! No one from the staff even bothered to come." Yet, the badger never called to let the parish office know. It's better to attack.

Sad to say, it does seem more and more to be a phenomena of our society to attack. We see this today in road rage, anger, people yelling at each other in a mall and, unfortunately, more and more through domestic violence. Each year, in March, I give the invocation at our chamber meeting when the mayor gives his state of the city address. Often the biggest increase in police calls has been that of domestic violence. In this area, as in many other cases, past hurts or past angers can cause the badger to attack. It is essential for the badger to look and see if feelings of rage, toward another, come from such incidents.

Another aspect of the badger's personality can reflect that part of our society which says, "I messed up, now you fix it for me!"

Our western mentality again comes into play here as often the badger becomes a victim. If there is anytime a parish needs to bring itself back to Eucharist and prayer it is when we find ourselves saying we are a victim. Yes, we can at times be a victim of insidious things that happen in our society. But we can never forget that the real victim is the one who hung upon the cross and gave His life for our sins. The badger, and anyone who feels they have been a victim, can never forget this important sacrificial element of Eucharist. Jesus is the real victim because we fail to open ourselves up to His Father's Kingdom.

It's similar to when we were kids and didn't do our homework. "Can I copy yours?" I messed up, but you fix it and if you don't I become a victim and attack. Or we tell a lie and we expect someone else to cover it up. I messed up, but someone should fix it, and if not, the badger attacks. We schedule a day with too much in it. The phone rings on the way out, the kids need something for their project tomorrow, the baby's crying, and we expect everyone to get out of our way. And if they don't, and fail to fix our situation, well, only one thing—attack! attack! attack!

Unfortunately, as the badger shows up in the various relationships of our lives, it can even attack one's own self. So many people will "badger themselves" for very innocent feelings. A person has a loved one pass away or a couple may have divorced. Only after one enters the normal, human process of healing, which involves anger, denial, bargaining, depression, guilt and other emotions, can healing come about. However, a song is heard, Thanksgiving comes, Christmas soon follows, the anniversary of death shows up on the calendar or a favorite spot is passed by in travel. Sometimes, a person will then say, "I thought I was doing so well," or, "I thought I was over it?"

You see, it is easy to badger ourselves. Feelings will always arise when memories emerge in our lives. Rather than badgering ourselves, we need to enter into the healing process at a deeper level. At this time God is calling us to a greater awareness of His promise not to abandon us. When a person has these normal feelings, it is not the time to "badger oneself." Another period of growing in God's trust has simply presented itself. In the end, we may often be our own worst enemy.

Finally, not only are humans liable to be attacked by the badger: God Himself can also be the target!

"God, you have to help me pass this exam—I can't flunk!" Of course, I didn't study but God has to fix it for me—and if not, well, what else---attack!

Or we await results of a medical exam and God had better come through with good results.

A young boy is said to have gone to see Santa Claus and tell him what he wanted for Christmas. After telling Santa he wanted a computer game, a bike, a wagon, a ball, a bat and numerous other things, Santa asked him if he had been a good boy. "Well," he said! "Can we just settle for the computer game!"

The boy was honest. He didn't try to have Santa fix his situation and attack. He knew Santa had made him admit some things he otherwise may not have. Rather than attack and attack, he took the consequences for his actions.

One wonders why people attack if you look at them the wrong way or happen not to say good morning to them. At times they may be right—we were too concerned with our own narrowness; however, often it is a result of past angers and hurts or a failure to take responsibility for one's own actions that results in their attacking.

I remember visiting a parishioner in a hospital and on my way out the lady at the front desk stopped me. "Are you Father Kraig?" she asked. "Yes," I answered. "I thought so," she said. "I'm a good friend of your parents and I saw you come in, but you looked really taken up in your thoughts, and I didn't want to bother you!"

There are times, as we see from that example, that members of the parish staff can, and should, be brought to accountability for their actions. While the lady at the hospital was not attacking me, her concern was a valid one. She was right! I was wrong. I was too taken up with myself to even notice her and that obviously came across. At times the badger can get testy and at times they have a right to. By and large, however, ministers of the church are trying to do the best job they can: to serve God and His people.

While my nephew tells me there are less and less badgers in the jungle, we may see more and more signs of them in the church as we move into a new millenium But more about their number at the end of this chapter. Where we might see them appear is when parishes lose a priest due to the priest shortage. And whether we want to admit it or not, there are less and less priests to serve God's people. In the Diocese of Cleveland, there were just under 600 active priests with 240 of them under age 40 in 1970. In 1999, active priests number 366 with 44 being under age 40. In talking to priest friends of mine throughout the country, this seems to be a consistent trend in many dioceses.

Often, a parish is used to having two priests. However, a new pastor is assigned and the parish is cut to one priest. As a result, it becomes necessary to cut the mass schedule. The elements are all there for a badger to go to work.

"But Father Jim always had two morning masses and five masses on the weekend. Who do you think you are to come in here and change things?" This is certainly a good question and an inquiry that could get us into so many other issues facing our church today, like: Communion Services and Priestless Sundays; married clergy; women priests and former priests returning to active ministry. However, those concerns are certainly not within the realm and scope of this book.. Sufficient to say, the badger can attack in these situations without knowing the total picture once again.

Whenever the badger shows itself in parish life, the staff and community needs to draw him or her back to the Eucharist, and prayer, and strive to involve them more fully in the entire parish picture. Perhaps the prayer of the community can lead to healing; talking about past hurts may also help. Or perhaps, making an inner healing retreat becomes part of the process.

Many churches are reaching out to those who, whether a badger or not, have been hurt by the church. It may have been something a priest, religious or lay person said that was offensive and caused them to leave. However, programs such as "Come For Another Look", "Welcome Home" and similar ones are all attempts to tell those, who have been hurt, they are welcome back to the Table of the Lord.

The badger obviously helps us recognize that at times we don't see the bigger and wider picture. I know myself, that when the first nice day in March comes, I call our councilman and ask when are the tennis nets going up. It doesn't matter that there might be sewer problems or there's a water backup. My needs are more important. When are the tennis nets going up?

In the end we can say the badger certainly calls us to see whether we are examining the total picture, and have all the facts, before we act. And when their attacks are justified, as many have been on me, they help us see the beauty of God's forgiveness in the sacrament of reconciliation. For the most part, I don't believe people get up in the morning and say: "Let's see, now, who can I hurt today?" But as humans, there are times we do hurt others, especially our own loved ones, and as a result we need to ask for forgiveness.

But what is fascinating to know about the badger is that they draw us towards kindness and charity. While the badger is a ferocious animal, less and less of them are in the jungle since they are often hunted for their fur. Perhaps the "badger mentality" and their attacks can likewise be destroyed as they see more and more of God's love and compassion from others. This is certainly a major challenge for anyone, but when you consider the "badger mentality" can show its sharp teeth at anytime, in any of us, it becomes a little easier.

In the fifteenth chapter of Matthew we read the following story:

> "Then Jesus went from that place and withdrew to the region of Tyre and Sidon. And behold, a Cananite woman of that district came and called out, 'Have pity on me, Lord, Son of David! My daughter is tormented by a demon.' But he did not say a word in answer to her. His disciples came and asked him, 'Send her away, for she keeps calling out after us.' He said in reply, 'I was sent only to the lost sheep of the house of Israel.' But the

woman came and did him homage, saying: 'Lord, help me.' He said in reply: 'It is not right to take the food of the children and throw it to the dogs.' She said, 'Please Lord, for even the dogs eat the scraps that fall from the table of their masters.' Then Jesus said to her in reply, 'O woman, great is your faith! Let it be done for you as you wish.' And her daughter was healed from that hour."
(Mt. 15:21-28)

For some reason or another I think Jesus and the woman in the above passage really enjoyed the presence and company of one another. I can't help but believe that she and Jesus "badgered" each other in a good-natured way. In the case of Jesus, His "badgering" tells us how much he wants to enter into our lives. And on the part of the woman, she shows that her "badgering" reflected the importance of persevering in our relationship with Jesus. Truly, one can never give up, especially in prayer, doing good, and coming to know our loving and forgiving God.

Badgers, too, help us realize how important it is to center our parish life around Eucharist and prayer. Otherwise, we may only strive to meet their needs in an effort to please them and, in doing so, ignore the needs of the entire faith-community. To desire to meet the needs of all, is, in my humble opinion, unhealthy. It is first of all impossible, and, to do so, may cause the minister to burn out. Then, he or she is unable to use his or her God-given talents for the betterment of the entire community. Secondly, one may give every effort possible to please all; however, in the end, is it being done for the minister's own self-gratification?

Next to my phone in my office there is an icon of Jesus entering Jerusalem on a donkey. I keep it there because of a story I once read. It seems that an old man and a young boy had a donkey, and one day, while out with it, people noticed the young man was riding the donkey and the old man walking next to it. "How rude," some people remarked "that the boy would let the old man walk." So the old man and the boy switched, the boy now walking and the old man riding the donkey. After about five minutes, some other people commented: "How ridiculous for the old man to ride. He should let the young boy ride since the boy is the future of the world. He has hopes, ideals and is versed in all kinds of new knowledge. Besides, the old man has lived his life." Since this was said, both decided to ride the donkey. About a half a mile later the donkey collapsed from the weight of both and died. And of course there's a simple moral to the story: Try to please everyone and you're gong to lose your donkey.

Individually, we cannot be all things to all people. However, may we grasp the fact that together, united with Jesus in the gift of Eucharist, we can be to each other what He wants us to be. If we stay centered in Jesus, in the Eucharist, we know He is all things to all peoples.

CHAPTER 6

THE HYENA

One of the things that sports fans in the Cleveland area are excited about is the new Cleveland Browns football team. Many others, and I, were obviously disappointed when the Browns moved in 1995 and took up residence in Baltimore. And yet, as football fans of the area await the beginning of a new era in Cleveland football, they have many vivid memories of exciting games at the old Cleveland Municipal Stadium.

One of the things that strikes me, as I recall watching some of the Browns' old games, is something that happens to anyone who watches their favorite football team play, whether professional, college, high school, or CYO. Whenever the team I was rooting for would score a touchdown, intercept a pass, or make a great play, you would hold your breath when you saw a yellow penalty flag on the field. Even if you didn't see it, you would still look around for them. And if there was one, it was a sign maybe all was not as well as it seemed. The play could stand or it could be called back. Suddenly, feelings of great elation could turn into disappointment.

As a matter of fact, some television networks now have the word "flag" in bold yellow under the score in the corner of the screen whenever there is a penalty on the play. Right away you know there is a potential problem. Announcers will immediately caution their listeners and say: "There's a flag on the play!"

This example comes to mind as I reflect on the hyena. While it is an animal whose habitat is in Africa, they are present in our parishes. I am told hyenas make a lot of noise, sometimes a squawking sound, or, as we have come to know, a laughing one.

Thus the term "laughing hyena." Laughter is always good to hear. Even though a good chuckle is healthy, the laughter of a hyena, who travels in packs is very aggressive and would cause one to turn back. It is known that a group of hyenas can even chase lions away. While they can have an "attacking mode" about them, we will concentrate on the 'laughing' aspect that seems to draw attention to themselves and causes one to reverse directions.

Just as yellow penalty flags signal caution after a big play, so, too, in a parish, a hyena, at first, appears to be a person whom you are glad to meet when you first come into contact with them. They make you happy to be a part of the parish community, but soon turn that initial welcomed feeling into one of hesitancy.

The hyena thus makes you look for the yellow penalty flag and cautions you to wonder if everything is as good as it sounds or appears.

Perhaps a story will help to get the point across. A frog was watching birds migrating south during the fall season. He was fascinated at how they could fly and wished he could go with them, to get away from the pending winter weather. He asked the birds how they flew but felt sad when he discovered that he, unlike the birds, had no wings. However, after putting his brain to work, he approached two birds with the following proposition: "What if I got a stick and the two of you put it in your beaks, and as you fly,

I'll just get in the middle and hang on to the stick with my mouth. That way I could fly south with you!"

The birds discussed the idea and agreed it was worth the try. And so the frog hung onto the stick with his mouth and, lo and behold, he was flying south. In fact, he was enjoying the trip very much. Some people happened to notice the frog flying with the birds and shouted up: "What a wonderful idea! Whoever thought of that?" Without hesitating, or missing a beat, the frog opened his mouth and said, "It was my idea, my idea!" And upon opening his mouth he fell to the earth and crashed.

The hyena very innocently needs to talk about himself, his accomplishments and be heard by others. One of the first signs of the yellow penalty flag occurs when you initially go to a church, whether that be a new assignment, a wedding, a funeral, a First Communion, a Baptism, or any sacramental need. The hyena appears: "Hi, father! I'm John Doe and I've been a member of the church since it first started. I, and a group of people, helped build this church and, with the help of a few others, were responsible for its funding when we ran the building campaign." Yellow penalty flags everywhere. While John may be very pleasant and sincere, this welcoming has, at times, been an attempt to convey the notion that he is important in the life of the parish. And because he has raised money for the building project, he may be trying to get across the point that his approval is necessary for important decisions.

A good priest friend of mine, in another state, had an experience which was charged with much electricity and emotion. Upon arriving at a parish, which had a communion rail, he decided to take it down, citing the fact that he was only doing what the church asks us to do. Needless to say this stirred a lot of feelings, and, as he mentioned to me, especially from those who, at first, were very welcoming and who had told him how instrumental they were in the running of the church. Because they had invested much time in the construction of the church, they were of the opinion they should also control the liturgy and what took place within the church building.

These are always difficult issues. We will see, as we progress through this chapter, that it is especially challenging since the hyena is often a well-intentioned individual who loves his church.

In many ways, it is similar to a gift one gives at Christmas time. Have you ever been involved in an exchange of gifts where someone says: "Open the gift now." And yet often a person wants to wait until Christmas to open it. The person giving the gift means well, but once the gift is given it no longer is in the possession of the giver. He must give up control of it. Now, it is up to the person to do what he wants with the gift.

If we take that analogy further, is that not what God did in giving us the great gift of Jesus and Eucharist. We are free to accept this gift and let Jesus be the center of our parish and our lives or we are free to reject the gift. Jesus never forces Himself upon us. You never have to look for yellow penalty flags with Jesus. His love, forgiveness, healing and eternal life are given to us freely and unconditionally.

Many people have worked selflessly and dedicated many hours of their time to make parish communities viable and Spirit-filled. A great deal of what we do today and much of our ministry is due to the fact that many have gone before us and laid the foundation. There is no doubt in my mind they will have a high place in God's Kingdom. So often, unfortunately, appreciation has been lacking for them. It is important for ministers to express their thanks to those who have made so many churches what they are today. However, as true as the accomplishments of the hyena are, so, too, is another side of the coin. And that is simply this: for some, you can never give them enough thanks and appreciation. They will be the first ones to tell you of their successes and their role in the parish's achievements. When they do, you can't help but think of

Mother Teresa who said, "I am not called to be successful. I am called to be faithful to the gospel of Jesus!"

The hyenas have done a great deal of good for the church and, in many ways, are the backbones of the church. What takes away from their accomplishments, however, is they can never get beyond telling others about their efforts, something which can affect each and every one of us. And it will happen to any minister or parish community when people forget it is God's power and presence in the gift of Eucharist that has brought about any good. Organizations, ministers and individuals are only God's instruments. When we fail to comprehend this simple fact, we, whether parishioner, organization or minister, will only hinder the presence of God in the community's prayer and celebration of Eucharist. Similar to the frog in the story of the birds, we will be drawing attention to ourselves rather than the tremendous power of God.

The result is simple. When we rely on our power more than God's, we will do all we can to make sure we do not lose it. Once we believe we have control, we hate to give it up.

Hyenas have developed in Africa and have moved very little outside of that country. However, many with a hyena mentality in parish life can, and, thank God have, progressed beyond themselves by letting go of their accomplishments to assist the parish in centering itself around prayer and Eucharist. They have let go of their desire to control. Some have become a Eucharistic Minister and bring the Body of Christ to those in hospitals and nursing homes; others as a lector or member of the RCIA team; others, in helping to feed the homeless; and still others as active participants in the various commissions such as liturgy, finance, evangelization or long-range planning. If, however, they do not move out of "their territory," they can become harmful to the life, growth and prayer of the parish by talking about the past rather than seeing parish needs which come from the community's prayer.

When people let God be the God of their lives, rather than their achievements, I think of the Magi who were asked, in a dream, to go back by a different route after following the star.

> "And having been warned in a dream not to return to Herod, they departed for their country by another way." (Mt. 2:12)

When the hyena allows Jesus to become Lord of the parish rather than the past, he can certainly face the future in the present moment, even if called to go via different routes; ones that are not familiar to us.

Someone once said the word "I" is the most boring word in the dictionary. I (there it is) guess there's some truth to that. It really can be boring to sit down and hear a person tell you how good their golf game is or all they've done. But talk about the Lord in a genuine, authentic way or how you've seen God's power working in your life and you'll see a different conversation. You can see it in a person's eyes, "Tell me more about this God! Tell me more about His healing power!" People are searching for the Lord and the hyena can often hinder that process with an "I" mentality.

Somewhere in my ministry I heard a story about a couple searching for a church to join. Among the many congregations they visited, one said they had just built a center with racquetball courts; another mentioned they have numerous organizations that meet regularly; still another stated how they had grown over the years. Disillusioned, they tried one final congregation who shared they have the Word of God and the Gift of Eucharist. Immediately, they joined.

Hopefully, we live our lives becoming more aware of the power of God in us and bringing others to that awareness in their lives.

"A city set on a mountain cannot be hidden. Nor do they light a lamp and then put it under a bushel basket; it is set on a lampstand, where it gives light to all in the house. Just so, your light must shine before others, that they may see your good deeds and glorify your heavenly Father." (CMT. 5: 146-16).

Jesus told us to let our light shine. However, it is to be a light that gives glory, honor and praise to our God. When we are more concerned about ourselves, our group or what we've done, rather than how God has touched our lives, or our parish community, we are doing a disservice not only to our God but also to the entire family of God.

I remember sitting down with an organization as they told me what they had done and then being presented with their schedule of events and speakers for the coming year. I then asked a question. "What makes this organization different from the local Kiwanis Club? What makes this organization unique to differentiate it from the local Chamber?" What I was getting at is that somehow, someway, people should be able to look at a schedule of events or accomplishments in a parish organization and say, "This is a Catholic group! They believe in prayer! They believe in Eucharist! They are committed to the Lord's ways and how God is leading them! They believe in the healing power of God! They believe in forgiveness!"

If this kind of observation is going on, by one outside the community, it is because parish meetings have begun with true prayer; time has been spent by the community in the presence of the Blessed Sacrament; time has been spent by the staff in prayer, discerning the ways of God; staff, commissions, and members of the parish have seen God's presence manifested through prayer;

and finally, the Sunday Eucharistic celebration has given people hope that God is the God of parish life and not an individual or an organization.

A hyena personality can not only affect our parish, but also our daily lives. As one begins a new job, he or she can be greeted by another and told how he has helped the company grow. However, when the newly employed asks for some initial help from that person, the veteran employee fails to lend a helping hand since it will not bring any personal benefit. In addition, companies can be hindered from growth and progress because one is always talking about the past rather than looking toward the future.

Likewise, the hyena can infiltrate family life. When I was involved with youth, I remember a teenager becoming addicted to drugs and alcohol. While he and his parents were in my office, the father, naturally upset, kept telling his son that he had given him a car, a stereo, anything he wanted. Finally, the boy just shouted out: "But you never gave me love!"

It may also be difficult to escape the hyena within the sacrament of marriage. How often, in counseling, a minister will hear one spouse say to another, "After all I have done for you!" "I can't believe you would feel this way since I have sacrificed so much to make this marriage work!" And yet, does a husband or wife make a marriage work according to their perspective or do they seek to grow together in God's graces? Does one strive to create a home or just a house to live in? It is easy to be efficient in our roles; however, above that, we need to be instruments of God's graces to one another.

Steve Warner, a country music artist, once sang a song entitled, "WHAT I DIDN'T DO" (Steve Warner Greatest Hits, 1987 MCA Records, Inc.). In the song he tells about a wife who divorces her husband, not so much for what he did but for what he didn't do. If the hyena has not moved beyond bringing attention to himself in marriage, it is easy to see how a situation can become, "It's not what I did, it's what I didn't do." Likewise, in parish life, if people are constantly calling attention to themselves and their organization, they will hinder the parish not so much for what they have done but for what they are now failing to do.

People who care about God's kingdom, and sharing His power and healing, are people you want to be around. There's a charisma about them! They radiate a joy; they convey a certitude and confidence in their actions! They believe Jesus is the Lord of their parish and their life, rather than a person's accomplishments or an organization's doings. There is a sense of "other centerdness" in their lives. Often, you just want to say, "Don't stop, tell me more! Tell me about this parish, tell me more how God is working within your community and the church!"

Polish music has always been a part of my life and I have been able to use my accordion talents on numerous occasions at various parish settings. I have played with some polish polka bands and have done a lot of what is called "jamming." Jamming is a term we use to get some musicians together -- an accordion player, a concertina player, a trumpeter, a drummer, a base player, and we just play one song after another. I love it! It's just pure fun. One of the musicians shouts out a song, the key it's in and we go from one to another. There comes a time we know we should quit but we keep saying, one more, one more!"

That analogy tells me a little about the hyena and what they offer us. By what hyenas fail to do, they call us to use our talents and gifts for the benefit of the entire parish. And just as you can't "jam" by yourself, you can't build a parish with just one group or with just one person. You need the gifts and God-given talents of all. When all work together, not caring who gets credit, everything is done for God's honor and glory. When all unite themselves in prayer around the Eucharist and not their past, then parish life happens. Then God becomes real. Then we want to say, "One more time, one more time, tell me more!"

Just as children need the example and love of parents, so, too, people looking for Jesus need to see a parish community that believes in prayer and Eucharist. Perhaps the hyena asks us the simple question, "Am I more concerned with bringing my glory, my kingdom, my organization, my accomplishments, or simply God's kingdom, God's gifts, God's talents?" The tragedy for any of us when we take on the hyena mode is that, in holding on to what we believe is so precious, we fail to see the beauty of God's kingdom with people of various personalities, gifts and talents who pray and discern God's will.

As I mentioned earlier, my nephew is an outdoors person. He loves nature. If he had his way he'd live his entire life outdoors. In discussing the hyena with him, he brought out an interesting point. He mentioned they have a tremendous sense of hearing and smell. In our own personal lives, a real danger to our spiritual growth is to withdraw when we hear of something we feel is threatening us. Likewise, when we get the feeling, or "smell out" change is needed, we can similarly retreat. If I get involved in this or that I'll have to give up what I enjoy doing. An example of this in parish life could be when one hears that a prayer group or some other activity might be starting.

Because it is perceived that what is new might take away from his or her organization and its accomplishments, a defensive feeling arises. Again, sad to say, hyenas close themselves up to the workings of God in their life and the parish.

Personally, working with the hyena is a real challenge but very rewarding, and at times fun, despite the fact that they sometimes make you see the yellow penalty flag. In many ways they have helped me grow in my priesthood. Often, they are part of the foundations or beginnings of a parish community and are able to provide a good history of a place. Sometimes you just have to put the fact that they always include themselves or their organization in the history of the parish on the back burner. They feel deeply for their parish community and in many ways have helped me appreciate a parish much quicker, than I would have, if they had not been around. But some simply continue to live in the past. While part of celebrating Eucharist is to recall how "Christ has died," the remainder is that "Christ is risen, Christ will come again!" Thus we celebrate how Jesus is acting now; and celebrating His presence in the present moment, we know we can look forward to what lies ahead.

It is very easy to think the parish exists only in our particular time; but there is a past as well as a present to each and every parish. Growth occurs when we not only discover but absorb its rich traditions. In becoming aware of them, The Tradition of Eucharist allows us to be more open to the workings of the Spirit of Jesus. As a result, the hyena allows us to look not only at our own individual talents, but those of the entire praying community to see how it can remain faithful to the gospel.

Probably one of the most important facets of the hyena's gifts is that they teach us not to take ourselves too seriously. They remind us that it is God's church and not mine. Many have come before us; many will come after us; through it all, the power of God and His graces will continue to guide His church. When all is said and done it is for Him that we minister. "Amen, I say to you, until heaven and earth pass away, not the smallest letter or the smallest part of a letter will pass from the law, until all things have taken place." (Mt. 5:18) The hyena thus does many things out of love. But, as we have seen, he can also do things out of self-love.

The idea of self-love was especially evident to me when a parishioner, with hyena characteristics, asked to use a space that was rented out. Somehow, for some reason or another, I knew there was a yellow penalty flag on the field when he made the appointment. When he saw me, his first words were, "I was wondering, Father, if you can cut me a deal with the rental of (the particular space)!"

And yet, while that "hyena mentality" can exist, we can only praise God that there are so many of God's people who just minister, volunteer, or help out because of one reason, and one reason only--their love and devotion to God.

Someone once said that the dangerous people in a parish are not those with ideas but those without ideas. The hyena certainly has ideas and probably is necessary in every parish. In one sense, we can be very thankful for them. But while one foot is in the past, we must also help him realize that another foot has to be in the present so that their experience and knowledge of the parish can assist the parish council, steering committee, or whomever answer God's call here and now. We cannot allow them to be like the anchor in the back of the boat. If one does not pull up the anchor the boat will be hindered from moving forward.

> "I was regretting the past and fearing the future." Suddenly my Lord was speaking: "My name is I am." He paused. I waited. He continued, "When you live in the past with its mistakes and regrets, it is hard. I am not there. My name is not I was. When you live in the future, with its problems and fears, it is hard. I am not there. My name is not I will be. When you live in this moment it is not hard. I am here. My name is I am."
> Helen Mallicoat

CHAPTER 7

THE SKUNK

Ah, the smell of a skunk! There's nothing quite like it anywhere. You can be driving, out jogging, taking a walk and suddenly that infamous odor hits you.

The skunk is obviously an animal you refrain from coming into contact with. Although my nephew tells me they are wonderful animals and that he actually got up close to one once, I'm not about to take his suggestion and try it. In fact, sometimes when I'm out jogging and get a strong whiff of the skunk, I immediately head inside. Call me a baby, say it's ridiculous but I want nothing to do with them. The skunk's spray has far reaching effects. On the highway, the scent can go on for miles.

Brian holds there is a certain beauty about skunks. But what is apparent from our human experience is that you want nothing to do with them. They breed a negativity and a negative reaction. Stay out of their path. Let them go their way, I'll go mine and let's hope we never encounter one another.

Perhaps my perception of the skunk is that it is an animal to avoid. Brian tells me the skunk won't spray unless he is afraid or needs to defend himself. When the skunk uses his spray, he then has to build up more resources. Basically, he is an animal with a limited amount of defense spray.

Even though the skunk is not a bad animal, people usually see it in a negative way. When you visit a zoo, you don't spend the same amount of time looking at each of the animals. One may get more attention and time from an individual and family than another. There are just some animals you find it difficult to be with and the skunk is one of them. Unlike the hyena whom you are thankful is in the parish, the skunk is one who fosters a negative perspective and can be a real detriment within the life of a parish striving to center its existence around prayer and the Eucharist.

Recently I went into a first grade classroom and after the usual, "Gooooood Morrrrrrrning, Faaaaaathhheerr," I asked them how school was going. They all responded very positively. I then questioned them as to how many liked reading and they all, without an exception, raised their hands. I proceeded to inquire how many liked recess, and once again received a similar response as did the subject of eating lunch. I next asked how many enjoyed writing and, again, all raised their hands. I thought, "hmmmm, they're raising their hands to anything I ask." So I asked them, "How many of you like trigonometry?" And you guessed it! They all raised their hands.

I laughed to myself, and probably a little out loud, but when I left I was happy to have had the opportunity to be around those first graders. There's something about them that no matter what kind of a day you are having, or how busy you might be, you're just glad to be with them. They are so uplifting, positive and special.

We need experiences like that. We live in a society where newspapers and the media thrive on the negative. As a result, we become oblivious to the good that comes about from people reaching out to our brothers and sisters. Many youth in our parishes are involved with worthwhile projects which affect and help the lives of numerous individuals. People in our faith-communities daily visit the sick and suffering in hospitals and nursing homes. Executives, business people and corporations in the business world continue to support organizations and people in need. While some desire publicity and make sure their efforts are known, there are still those who do so much behind the scenes. And yet, if you were to go strictly by the evening news, you might ask: "I wonder who shot whom today; in what city will we see the drug raid tonight? How old will the parent(s) be today who abandon their child? It'll be interesting to see who started a fire when the news comes on." Negativity, negativity, negativity! It is there from the moment we turn on the morning news until we go to bed. While it is said that the media is just bringing the facts and news to its people, we all know it is done because people thrive on negativity and ratings to bring in more advertising dollars. Unfortunately, the good and the positive never gets reported.

I share the above story of the first graders because they portray what the skunk is not. Unfortunately, the skunk's attitude conveys a stench to be avoided. You do not want to be around the skunk; unlike the first graders, you do not find the skunk uplifting at all. As a matter of fact, you simply want to withdraw and have nothing to do with the skunk.

It is said Charles Darwin was happiest when he had something to gripe about. One night, while he and his wife were guests at a banquet, he noticed everything was wrong. Dry speeches, terrible drinks, bad food, and, above all else, Darwin happened to be sitting in a draft. It was obvious he was not happy. You just had to listen to his complaints. Later on, Mrs. Darwin was asked for forgiveness by one of those hosting the banquet because he had noticed her husband was so terribly upset. Mrs. Darwin simply responded: "He had a wonderful time. He was able to find fault with everything!"

Who wants that kind of negativity around the parish community? The music is never right; if only they'd stress my opinion they would have more people attending their meetings; things aren't the way they used to be or the way they should be; parents just don't teach their kids anything anymore—when I was a parent my kids never...! Homilies are never good enough, sisters don't dress like nuns anymore, women are allowed in the sanctuary, lay people give out Communion, they're raising their hands when they pray, the church should get in touch with its people, the pastor is too busy to see me, bishops require an appointment to see them and you need connections to meet the pope. And why is the church reaching out to the gay person, the lesbian? These are just some of the statements that you "smell" when the squirt comes from the skunk.

They might, in a gracious act of concession, allow the social concerns group to go and feed the poor once a month! Just don't expect them to help.

When challenged, they will spray an odor of negativity; but since a skunk only has so much squirt, they'll simply walk away if someone confronts them about their ideas. Skunks do not want anyone in their space. But once they are refueled, watch out! Beware! The great whiff begins and negativity is present once again.

Come the Christmas and Easter season the skunk will scowl at those who come only twice a year to church. Rather than saying "Good morning, glad to have you praying with our community," it is better for the skunk to have a negative attitude and say something like, "Won't see them again until next year!" To make things worse, the person who comes on Easter and Christmas parks in the usual space the skunk has, and, to top it off, sits in the pew normally occupied by the skunk.

The attitude of Jesus was certainly much different toward a person who was judged as sinful or not worthy to be in the presence of another. In Jn. 8:1-11 we read:

"Jesus went to the Mount of Olives. But early in the morning he arrived again in the temple area, and all the people started coming to him, and he sat down and taught them. Then the scribes and the Pharisees brought a woman who had been caught in adultery and made her stand in the middle. They said to him, 'Teacher, this woman was caught in the very act of committing adultery. Now in the law, Moses commanded us to stone such women. So what do you say?' They said this to test him, so that they could have some charge to bring against him. Jesus bent down and began to write on the ground with his finger. But when they continued asking him, he straightened up and said to them, 'Let the one among you who is without sin be the first to throw a stone at her.' Again he bent down and wrote on the ground. And in response, they went away one by one, beginning with the elders. So he was left alone with the woman before him. Then Jesus straightened up and said to her, 'Woman, where are they? Has no one condemned you?' She replied, 'No one, sir.' Then Jesus said, 'Neither do I condemn you. Go, [and] from now on do not sin any more.'"

Jesus could have had a negative attitude toward the woman, joined in with the crowd and judged her; but His Father's kingdom of reconciliation and accepting all, as children of the Father, was more important. It is interesting that Jesus waited until the crowd dispersed to speak to the woman. As we mentioned earlier, the skunk is a negative animal and, once it squirts, refuels and sprays again. Talking to the woman in front of the people would have probably precipitated more animosity and criticism, not only towards Jesus but, the woman also. By waiting until the crowd goes away, Jesus avoids more negativity and judging.

If a community centers itself around prayer and the Eucharist, is not the time of Christmas and Easter a special opportunity where both staff and community can reach out to those who only come at that time of the year? Perhaps some have been hurt by the church, staff or parishioners. Rather than spraying them with negativity, an approach that affirms with compassion, understanding and the forgiveness of Jesus would be much better. Unfortunately, since negativity can breed negativity, a staff or parish can get caught up in it, and take on the nature and spray of the skunk by not allowing a Christmas or Easter Catholic to feel welcome.

The fact that you want to get away from the negativity and whiff of the skunk is completely contradictory to what the Eucharist is about. The Body and Blood of Jesus should bring people together into a praying community. Staff and parishioners must always remember that Eucharist is a sign of unity rather than a sign to avoid one another.

Our Holy Father, Pope John Paul II, has spoken on numerous occasions about the essential call all have to reach out and evangelize. His encyclical, "Redemptoris Missio," proclaimed three objectives of mission: To proclaim the Gospel to all people, to help bring about the reconversion of those who have received the Gospel but live it only nominally, and to deepen the Gospel in the lives of believers (no. 33). Earlier on, in that same document, John Paul further declared, "I sense that the moment has come to commit all of the Church's energies to a new evangelization and to the mission ad gentes. No believer in Christ, no institution of the Church, can avoid this supreme duty: to proclaim Christ to all peoples" (No. 3).

On two occasions, I have been made aware of how people came back to the church at Christmas and Easter through the warm reception they had from a parish community. One particular instance that stands out is when a father, whom we will call Larry, approached me after an Easter Sunday celebration. Larry commented on the welcome he felt not only from the pulpit, but also the people of the community. As a result, he decided to reexamine his own faith commitment and to look into the possibility of getting his boys baptized. To this day, it is always rewarding to see Larry and his sons at church and sharing their faith within their community. That kind of welcome, more than the negativity of the skunk, can only help to bring about The Holy Father's desires.

God's power is greater than any sense of negativity. Sometimes I wonder how many times Jesus wanted to get negative and say things like, "Peter, you just don't understand! How can you be so foolish? Grow up and get a life!" Or, in the Gospel of Mark, after the recording of many healings and miracles in the first six chapters, Jesus feeds the five thousand (Mark 6:34-44). Immediately after that, he walks on the water (Mark 6:45-52) while the apostles, in great fear, are being tossed about in the boat. What a time to once again say something similar to, "You guys never learn, do you? Do you really think I'd abandon you?" Instead, he only says, "Take courage, it is I, do not be afraid." (Mark 6:50b) Always, however, His Father's Kingdom takes precedence as we hear in the Garden of Gethsemenee, "My Father, if it is possible, let this cup pass from me; yet, not as I will, but as you will." (Mt. 26:39) And finally, on the cross, the ultimate, "Father, into your hands I commend my spirit." (Lk. 23:46)

Jesus obviously saw something greater than negativity. He didn't just turn a negative into a positive. Rather he knew that nothing, no force on earth, nothing, nothing was greater than His Father's Kingdom. No person or group of people anywhere could take Him away from His primary mission—to bring His Father's love and reconciliation to all people.

Surrendering to the Father, as Jesus did, is perhaps what we are left to do in dealing with a person who takes on a skunk's personality. We can only give them to the Lord in prayer. Trying to engage the skunks in a rational discussion is next to impossible. They want to remain negative and no matter what the staff, the church or pastoral minister says, they've dismissed themselves from being wrong. One of my faults early in my priesthood was to think I could bring a skunk out into the daylight. That statement in itself is full of pride, as only God's graces will lead to a change of heart. However, that is one of the things that a skunk helps us recognize. Namely, that God, and only God, can bring about conversion.

This has become evident to me, and I'm sure to any minister, on numerous occasions. In talking to other priests and pastoral ministers, we have commented on how we had a homily or presentation we thought would change the world. However, it bombs out. Why? Could it be we depended more on ourselves than God's graces? On the opposite side, we can feel we have a program or talk where something just isn't right. Yet people come and tell us how much they got out of it. Again, it is not we and our words that lead to conversion. In the end, God's graces will touch the hearts of believers and ultimately the skunk.

Another example of God's graces touching people is an experience many have had, whether they are active in parish ministry or not. It is simply those occasions when we spent time with people listening to their experiences. Afterwards, it is not uncommon to receive a letter from them, or run into them, and be informed how much our presence helped them through their crisis. And all one did was listen. God's graces are truly incomprehensible.

One of my joys at Saint John Neumann is to occasionally celebrate the Heart of the Living Water Charismatic Mass on the first Friday of the month. While I have received much growth from this Mass and the prayer of the people present, on one occasion it provided me with the realization that you cannot engage a skunk in a rational discussion. Once a person said they were thinking of attending the mass. When that was overheard by the skunk, the stench was evident. "You're not going to that nonsense, are you?" When challenged about his comment, the person continued to make negative comments about the charismatic mass. Once again the spray of the skunk emerged as negativity spewed from his thoughts about the charismatic movement within the church.

Saint John Neumann has been blessed with a number of powerful prayer ministries. Our lay involvement in various prayer groups is truly a gift from God for which I am very grateful. The praying and healing ministries, through the intercession of Mary, the mother of Jesus, and our patron saint, John Neumann, have seen much healing brought to many individuals. In an earlier chapter (the Rabbit) I mentioned how we have had letters from doctors who could give no reason why cancer in a person was no longer present. In addition, others, who have been prayed over, have told me and members of the praying ministry how they experienced healing. One case in particular stands out among many.

A few years ago, Jerry told me his mother, who lived in another state, was dying. The doctor contacted him to come and see her if he wished to be with her when she died. Our praying ministry gave him the novena to St. John Neumann and we kept his mother, as well as him, in our prayers. To this day, three or four years later, Jerry's mother continues to serve the Lord through her life. The power of God, through prayer in a parish, is truly icredible.

The people involved in these ministries believe they are called to this ministry. They know the reason for miracles is to give God glory. They are convinced healing happens in peoples' lives because of God. Their faith tells them there is power in prayer and they know where two or three are gathered, the Lord is present.

They believe in the powerful God of healing, the powerful God of love, the powerful God of forgiveness.

Unfortunately, there'll always be one skunk who will say something like, "Oh, yeah! If God can heal, why didn't he do this or that in my life?" And after he shoots that spray, he refuels again, with another zinger, "Oh, that's a bunch of nonsense!" (I have heard other words used instead of nonsense.)

As we said earlier, there are certain animals in the zoo that make it difficult to be in their presence, and, obviously from the above, pose a great challenge to engage in conversation.

It is a shame the skunk only breeds negativity as there are, and can be, legitimate concerns. But he simply cannot see the good and sacrifices others have made. Whereas the hyena helped us understand the past, the skunk is just negative about anything that has gone on within the parish community.

In the Prologue to the Gospel of John, we read some very beautiful words and some very sad words:

> "In the beginning was the Word,/ and the Word was with God,/ and the Word was God./ He was in the beginning with God./ All things came to be through him,/ and without him nothing came to be./ What came to be through Him was life,/ and this life was the light of the human race;/ the light shines in the darkness,/ and the darkness has not overcome it./ A man named John was sent from God. He came for testimony, to testify to the light so that all might believe through him. He was not the light, but came to testify to the light. The true light, which enlightens everyone, was coming into the world./ He was in the world,/ and the world came to be through him,/ but the world did not know him. He came to what was his own, but his own people did

not accept him. But to those who did accept him he gave power to become children of God, to those who believe in his name, who were born not by natural generation nor by human choice nor by a man's decision but of God./ And the Word became flesh/ and made His dwelling among us,/ and we saw his glory,/ the glory of the Father's only Son,/ full of grace and truth." (Jn 1:1-14)

God's Word, Jesus, came for life and as a light to the human race. As a nocturnal animal, the skunk obviously shields itself from light. When one fails to expose themselves to the Light of Christ, the darkness of negativity rises preventing one from recognizing the power of God in and through others.

During my ministry, I have been in three assignments where construction building took place. One particular conversation with a parent stands out.

"You guys built wrong!" She said. "You should have built more classrooms. We're gong to have more kids in the future." When I responded we needed what we built, her negativity continued.

"Who needs a gymnasium!" Again, I told her of a state law regarding physical education.

"What was wrong with were we had gym class" she continued?

"But, Maam," I answered, "are you aware how unhealthy it is to have lunch and gym in the same room?"

Again, more squirt. "Another thing, the proportion of 22 boys and 13 girls in the third grades is not good. It doesn't allow for equality among the boys and the girls!"

I know I should not have come back with what I said, but, like I mentioned earlier, you just don't want to be around a skunk. And so I said the following: "Maam, what do you want me to do? Have the boys get a sex-change?"

It certainly was not the way Jesus would have responded in His ministry but, as we have been saying, negativity breeds negativity.

When a community sees skunks among themselves it is important to continue to be faithful to God's word, the Eucharist and community prayer. In this way they keep their growth on a positive road and forge strong bonds in their commitment to the church and to one another. Eucharist provides hope and an awareness that God and others are with me. It is good to be in the presence and prayer of the community even though I, nor the community, have all the answers. But it is good to be with them because there is the bursting forth of a power greater than I, and all of us together, namely, the power of Jesus in the Eucharist. The one whose scent tends to scatter us cannot tear us away from what we are about.

Above all, the skunk helps us understand we may be wrong and have to admit it—but that's ok! Healing can now begin. It helps us realize that, "Yes, at times, we do have prejudices but that, too, is ok," as God's healing can only commence when we see the shadow side of ourselves.

This became especially clear to me when I became pastor of St. John Neumann Church in January of 1990. Previous to that time it was easy for me to be negative and critical of the institutional church. However, since becoming pastor, I have come to realize that many issues do not have simple solutions. In fact, if there is a simple solution it probably will not work.

Since learning this I have come to realize that there are issues within the institutional church which find me and the church at odds. But it is this same church that has provided me with the gift of Jesus and the gift of His forgiveness through the Eucharist. And this same church, with its many sinners, has also provided all of us with tremendous saints. Among the weaknesses of its members, there are men and women, in every age of the church, who have become saints through living and ministering among the Body of

Christ despite their beliefs, tensions, and disagreements with the institutional church. In many ways, the people of faith have saved me from growing and developing the outlook of a skunk.

One of the great challenges of the Easter gospels is Jn. 20:24-29.

> "Thomas, called Didymus, one of the Twelve, was not with them when Jesus came. So the other disciples said to him, 'We have seen the Lord.' But he said to them, 'Unless I see the mark of the nails in his hands and put my finger into the nailmarks and put my hand into his side, I will not believe.' Now a week later his disciples were again inside and Thomas was with them. Jesus came, although the doors were locked, and stood in their midst and said, 'Peace be with you.' Then he said to Thomas, 'Put your finger here and see my hands, and bring your hand and put it into my side, and do not be unbelieving but believe.' Thomas answered and said to him, 'My Lord and my God!' Jesus said to him, 'Have you come to believe because you have seen me? Blessed are those who have not seen and have believed.'"

The challenge of this gospel account is that there appears to be a skunk in the upper room, Thomas, or, as he has come to be known throughout the centuries, "Doubting Thomas." He seems negative about believing the resurrection of Jesus. In this account Jesus appears to the apostles in the upper room and Thomas is not with them. Perhaps, however, Thomas may be a hero as he calls us out of a skunk existence.

After being told that the disciples have seen Jesus, Thomas says he won't believe unless he puts his finger in the nailprints and his hand in the side of Jesus. Why is he called Doubting Thomas? If you've seen Jesus, then why, Thomas challenges the apostles, are you locked up in the upper room with your fears and anxieties and biases about those who seem to be coming after you? Maybe Thomas is proclaiming, "If you've seen Jesus, and believe, why aren't you out sharing the good news?"

In the Gospel account of the raising of Lazarus from the dead, after hearing Jesus say He is going up to Jerusalem to die, who said "Let us also go to die with him?" (John 11:16) It is Thomas. Is Thomas really "Doubting Thomas" or was he just among some skunks who were breeding negativity?

We can probably say, without hesitation, the skunk will continue its spray and continue to be with us. And if, at times, you wonder if the church would be better off without them, there is always the possibility that they, like the supposedly "Doubting Thomas," cause us to reflect on our lives, with the challenge: We are the Body of Christ! We are children of the Father who calls each and every one of us to His Kingdom through the teaching of Jesus. Similar to Thomas, who was with the other disciples in the upper room, we are with our brothers and sisters when we gather to celebrate Eucharist as a praying community. As we are among the Body of Christ we have to be able to say, like Thomas, to The Body of Christ 'My Lord and My God!' And not just once, but each and every time we are present at the Eucharistic celebration. "My Lord and My God! You, Jesus, are the Lord of the Church and the master of my life. Help my lack of faith to grow so I am not spraying a negative scent, but the good news of Jesus and His great gift of Eucharist."

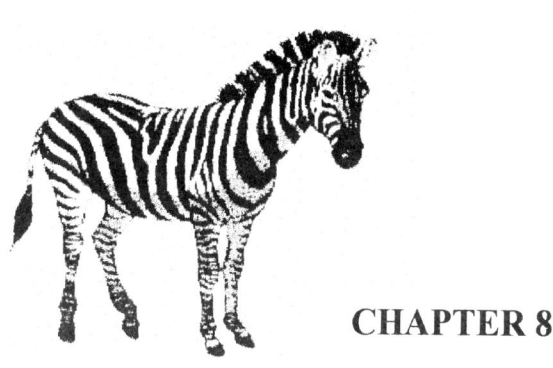

CHAPTER 8

THE ZEBRA

"Mommy! Daddy!" I remember shouting those words. It was horrifying. My heart was pounding, I wondered where I was; I was afraid to move any of my limbs wondering what I should do. Somehow, however, I managed to get enough strength to run down the hallway to my mother and father's bedroom.

I always remember that initial interruption to my childhood sleep. Zebras were coming at me and I still can see their black and white stripes. I can't recall what precipitated this or why it came about, but obviously I had my first nightmare as a child. Even now, when I am watching television, I will flip to another channel if zebras come on the screen. There's something about them I just don't like.

Maybe the nightmare was the hundreds of black and white stripes racing toward me; but somehow, I believe that if I view zebras for any amount of time, the initial nightmare will repeat itself when I go to bed. And even though I have avoided any visual contact with the zebra in books or on television, those ominous black and white stripes have manifested themselves both in my life and in my ministry.

The zebra, like the rabbit, not only expects things to be his way, but, in addition, the way they have always been. Unlike the rabbit, however, the zebra is willing to stay in the parish community and work for his strong beliefs and convictions. Because the zebra is dedicated to a particular faith community and committed to his or her perception of The Body of Christ, he or she brings a very defined and predictable stability to God's people. And the reason is this - for the zebra, there is no gray area. It's either black or white, the way it's always been and/or the way it will always be. In spite of their strong loyalty, however, conflicts are inevitable since their vision of the parish is often different from that of the entire parish community.

Unfortunately, with the zebra, it's either my way or no way. In terms of its exterior—it's either black or white.

One particular story about a husband and a wife brings out how a zebra mentality will close itself off to another's perspective. It seems a man had a problem drinking. One day, while reading the newspaper, he happened to come across an article which stated excessive drinking was dangerous for one's health. His wife, who had painstakingly tried to help him over the years, noticed him reading the article. "What do you think of that?" she asked. "It's a great article, he said. "I'm going to give up reading the newspaper."

Because the man was so set in his ways, an opportunity for personal growth was lost. Believing my perspective is the best is something I have to constantly guard against in my own life. At times, when I reflect on the fact that I have already lived over half my life, I find myself wondering what exactly is meant when someone says: "I can't wait until I retire!" There is obviously the desire to be free, to do what one likes to do and be more creative with one's time. I know, however, that when I catch myself saying those words, there is another side which says: (1) I don't want to keep up with all the advances in technology; (2) Let's keep things the way they are; and (3) better yet, let's keep things my way so I can maintain my own securities. In short, let's keep the zebra outlook—either black or white—my way or no way - and not rock the boat!

That kind of mentality only stifles one's personal growth. An example of how one can initially encounter a zebra in pastoral ministry might be, "You're charismatic, aren't you, Sister?" or, "Do you have a devotion to Mary, Father?" In other words, the zebra, with its black and white thinking, wants to know if you are with me or against me. How different this is from those who see the value of different types of prayer and various forms of spirituality and seek enrichment of their own lives by inquiring into how God works through others and in others.

Not only ministers of a parish community experience the zebra, but also organizations when they hear, "We've never done that in this parish! Our meetings always begin this way!"

Other zebras know exactly what will save the church.

- "You need to preach about Mary, Father!"
- "If you gave the old hell, fire and brimstone homilies the church would be much better."
- "When you start singing the old traditional songs that's when church attendance will increase!"
- "This church would be filled up if we had more spirit-filled music!"

It is, safe to say, a myopic vision; however, the zebra loves his church, believes in his God and wants others to experience God's blessings. The tragedy, however, is that their black and white thinking limits not only their own personal growth but that of the entire community.

This becomes evident when organizations within a parish have always had fund-raising events as their main objective like Monte Carlo weekends or Las Vegas nights. While these may attract a large number of people, a new member, or, the minister, might raise a few simple questions: "Is this really benefiting the entire community? How many present were actually from the parish?

Should alcoholic beverages be served?" Legitimate questions that challenge a group to consider whether its events serve the growth of the entire community or whether there is a need to maintain their image as a fund-raising group. Legitimate questions that could lead to other activities involving young as well as old and parents with their children. An event that would be more family-centered might make less money and thus cause a conflict with the zebra if he or she believes their organization has as its purpose to raise money. The black and white stripes emerge and a nightmare begins. Even though a parish may have a mission statement which clearly states the direction and vision of the parishioners, the zebra will cause a nightmare.

Liturgical ministers have also experienced how the zebra's outlook can limit the growth of the community. Throughout the church, the ministry of usher was to seat people for mass and to take up the collection. As the church looked at the celebration of Eucharist, this ministry, too, was seen from a different perspective. What many churches did was ask their ushers to take on a role of greeting the people and to seat people at appropriate times. This would avoid distracting the community during the Liturgy of the Word. Once the readings began people would no longer be seated as a courtesy to those listening to God's Word being proclaimed. Thus people could feel welcome when they walked into church and could hear God's word with complete attention. If the celebration of Eucharist is primary, and the community strives to center its life around God's Word, prayer and Eucharist, one can see how these developments in the ministry of usher would benefit the entire community. However, a nightmare of conflicts will arise if one in that ministry has the zebra mentality and feels the role of usher is to take up the collection and get people seated.

Many people who desire their way, however, have the good of the community at heart and realize their wishes and desires only stunt their growth as well as that of the praying community. One particular woman, coming from an early Sunday morning Mass, stands out. While very friendly and affirming, she said, "I wish we could sing the old songs; they really meant a lot to me. But since we don't I guess we'll have to learn the new ones!"

I reflected on what she shared with me. Although she desired Pre-Vatican II music, was she beginning to realize her desires were not always the best for the community? Eucharist and Jesus were obviously very important to her and from my perception she was a person who had placed her trust in the Lord throughout her life. Jesus sustained her in the past! Jesus would give her hope for the future. As a result the present moment could be lived and entered into through communion with Jesus and the faith community. Things were not the way she believed they should be. Yet, because of her belief in the prayer of the community, she could give thanks to God around the Table of the Lord with her brothers and sisters and be open to ways God was speaking to her, through music and prayer, contrary to her desires.

In the sixth chapter of Saint John's Gospel (Jn. 6:22-71) we read the well-known Bread of Life discourse. After we hear Jesus saying numerous times that 'he who eats His flesh and drinks His blood will have eternal life,' we read the following:

> "Then many of his disciples who were listening said, 'This saying is hard; who can accept it?'...As a result of this, many [of] his disciples returned to their former way of life and no longer accompanied him. Jesus then said to the Twelve, 'Do you also want to leave?' Simon Peter answered him, 'Master, to whom shall we go? You have the words of eternal life. We have come to believe and are convinced that you are the Holy One of God'".(Jn. 6:60,66-69)

Somehow the above mentioned woman makes you believe she would proudly speak up with Peter and say: "Lord, to whom shall we go—you have the words of eternal life!" Unlike the zebra mentality, (my way or no way—black or white) she can live with gray area, tensions and paradoxes that are part of a community centering itself around the Eucharist. Among these would be the desire to trust while we await the results of a medical exam—but will it turn out alright? The realization I must forgive but what about the bitterness in my heart? The knowledge I should reach out to my brother and sister less fortunate than I but yet the hesitancy to let go; the desire to serve our God mixed in with our own satisfaction. In becoming one like us through the Incarnation, Jesus took on every anxiety and tension that is a part of our life, and, in the human condition that we find ourselves, showed us how to live, not through "my way or no way," but, by trusting in His Father. As we bring these human tensions to the Lord's Table, we can take consolation in the words of St. Paul:

> "Three times I begged the Lord about this, that it might leave me, but he said to me, 'My grace is sufficient for you, for power is made perfect in weakness.' I will rather boast most gladly of my weaknesses, in order that the power of Christ may dwell with me. Therefore, I am content with weakness, insults, hardships, persecutions, and constraints, for the sake of Christ; for when I am weak, then I am strong.'" (2Cor. 12.8-10)

There are times in our lives where all we can do is turn to the grace of God. While that may appear weak to many of the world, it is then we become strong. And if we had all the answers and knew exactly how God should be directing His church, then why would we need the gift of faith?

The zebra simply exempts itself from any gray area or change; and yet, throughout the history of the church, teachings and practices of one era fade as another period approaches. Many liturgical reforms have obviously taken place through the ages and sacraments are celebrated much differently today compared to the late fifties.

In the early years of my priesthood, which I will elaborate on in the chapter, "The Squirrel," I had a zebra mentality, "I'm right, you're wrong, end of discussion!" That approach led to a reoccurrence of my nightmare. Thank God many people and situations eliminated those black and white stripes. One example comes to mind.

While out with a group of teenagers at a restaurant in the late seventies, I was very frustrated with a waitress. We were given what I thought was poor service. I felt she was rude and couldn't have cared less about her customers. I commented how we should leave her a penny tip to let her know our displeasure. After all, what I saw and experienced, had to be that of everyone else and I had to make my point. The zebra was at work and the youth had to learn how one stands up for what he believes in. One of the teens spoke up and said, "Father, did you ever think that the waitress might have just gone through a divorce, or that her children may be home sick or her husband just left her?" Even though I was speechless it was a good lesson. The way I see things is not always the way things are!

In discussing the zebra with my nephew, it was interesting to find out the zebra can be aggressive but is unable to be domesticated. How many households, families, marriages and parent/child relationships have seen their homes become simply a house where people live but share very little because of an aggressive, wild zebra mentality? The "my way or no way," black and white stripes, have caused people to give up hope for any growth in their marriage or family because a situation was impossible to discuss. "You just don't bring that up in his presence!" Or, "I know what her answer will be to that question before I even ask!" are just a few of the statements anyone who works with people has heard. The zebra mentality not only causes nightmares; it is also destructive.

How many marriages see two people just coexisting because both believe they are right and will not give in? How many marriages have suffered from an attitude of, "I'm right, you're wrong, end of discussion!" It is impossible for God's kingdom to emerge whenever that type of black and white zebra mentality is present. The nightmare only continues.

Although not that prevalent in today's church, the black and white stripes of the zebra often became visible when a Catholic married a Non-Catholic. As recent as the mid eighties, I remember a parishioner, whom we will call Paul, telling me very directly, without hesitation, and in no uncertain terms, that he would not attend his daughter's wedding because her fiancé was not of our faith. Despite his daughter's hurt, it was impossible to discuss the situation with him.

In addition to the Second Vatican Council's Decree on Ecumenism, there has been much healing and good will among ministers and people of various denominations. I know I have been present in Protestant churches and Protestant ministers have celebrated the sacrament of marriage with me in the Catholic Church. In addition, ministers in cities and suburbs meet regularly to discuss how churches in an area can witness to Jesus. While I felt sorry for Paul's daughter, it was more painful to see him keep a black and white approach which prevented God's graces from penetrating his life.

Interracial marriages can also cause the ominous black and white stripes to appear. I have seen family members disowned; thankfully, however, an attitude of acceptance and understanding is more the norm. Hopefully, we have come to the realization we are all children of God our Father.

> "But when the fullness of time had come, God sent his Son born of a woman, born under the law, to ransom those under the law, so that we might receive adoption. As proof that you are children, God sent the spirit of his Son into our hearts, crying out, 'Abba, Father!' So you are no longer a slave but a child, and if a child then also an heir, through God." (Galatians 4:4-7)

Wherever there is a zebra mentality, judgments will inevitably follow:
- "Kids are all the same—he's got to be on drugs!"
- "He's too old—what would he know?"
- "Ever since she came all we've had is changes—she just wants to do her own thing!"
- "Ever since he was born he could do nothing right—how can he ever amount to anything in life?"

Certainly there are times judgments are necessary for our growth and the betterment of others. We judge this school meets my child's needs better than another; we decide if a career move is good for my family; we assess driving conditions and make a judgment about proceeding to our destination. However, to inflict a judgment on a Child of God because of one's faith, race, beliefs, age or whatever, has no place in the church. The words of 1 Jn.3:1 ("See what love the Father has bestowed on us that we may be called the children of God. Yet so we are. The reason the world does not know us is that it did not know him") are certainly worthwhile for reflection in the life of any Christian, but especially the zebra. Otherwise the black and white stripes will produce another nightmare.

In the fall of 1994 I had the privilege of studying for three months in Rome with approximately forty priests from the United States. One professor, in particular, addressed the topic of The Kingdom of God at great length. Although I had used the term "Kingdom of God" many times in my preaching, it was still a very vague term. However, through his teaching, what became apparent to me is that one with a black and white stripe mentality cannot, and does not, understand how much Jesus desired to bring His Father's Kingdom to all people.

The professor pointed out that in the Gospel of Luke, Jesus shares numerous meals with many people. The table where Jesus ate had room for all, especially those considered as outcasts. More precisely, it was pointed out how:

(1) There is no room for judgment. (Lk. 10:38-42) Martha accuses her sister, Mary, of abandoning her since Mary is not in the kitchen helping her with the meal but rather listening to Jesus. Jesus responds by telling Martha she is concerned about many things and Mary has chosen the better portion in listening to Him.

(2) Jesus came to proclaim His Father's kingdom. (Lk 11:37-53). The Pharisees and scholars of the law believe externals, paying tithes, seats of honor in synagogues and obeying certain rituals will make one a good person in God's eyes. Jesus can only say "Woe to you" five times for that concept about one's relationship with God and for paying no attention to one's love for God.

(3) All are welcome around the Table of the Lord. (Lk 14:7-25) Jesus instructs the host that he should invite the poor, the crippled, the lame and the blind and, to emphasize the point, repeats the same in the parable of The Great Feast (Lk. 14:15-24). Those considered as outcasts are welcome at the table.

(4) God's love for all in unconditional. (Lk. 15:10-32) Here, in the passage of the Prodigal Son, (more appropriately called the Loving Father) the father welcomes his son back with no strings attached. In fact, he even throws a banquet.

From what we have said thus far, it is obvious that one with black and white zebra characteristics can choose to hear only what he or she wants to hear regarding the teachings of Jesus. For in the black and white, "my way or no way, we've always done it this way" approach there are: (1) judgments, (2) the heart is overlooked, (3) all are not welcome around God's table and (4) only certain people are worthy of God's love. Is it any surprise nightmares would occur?

While the zebra mentality has caused nightmares in the church, it is even more frightening to reflect on how the zebra, despite the guidance of the spirit in the church, will be present in communities during the years ahead. One of the many issues, for example, that confronts Roman Catholic Churches throughout our country is a just salary for its teachers. At the beginning of the 1998-99 school year, the Diocese of Cleveland began the year with 99 teacher vacancies. The Archdiocese of Detroit, (with 13,000 fewer students than Cleveland) had 340 vacancies and the Diocese of Newark, (with 7,000 fewer students), had over 200 vacancies. In addition, teachers throughout the country in Catholic Schools, have worked for, at times, $15,000.00-$25,000.00 less than their fellow-teachers at public schools.

Regarding this particular issue, even though teachers are entitled to a just salary, it is easy to see the nightmare a zebra will cause. "We never had to pay the amount of tuition they're paying today," he'll proudly boast. This is said despite the fact that a little over 90% of the teachers in Catholic Schools back in the fifties were religious, had taken a vow of poverty and were paid $50.00 a month. Today, 93% are lay people who are paid pennies above poverty and entitled to just benefits. If it's a black and white issue for the zebra, and should be done the way it's always been, a closed-minded approach is sure to follow as well as a nightmare.

In addition, predictions show that dioceses throughout our country will have less priests than parishes in roughly twenty years. What will ministry be like? How will liturgy be celebrated? Sacraments? What will PSR programs look like? What will the financial issues be for the church in those upcoming years? What will staffs be like? Will we have more than one couple getting married at a liturgy and more than one family present for a funeral?

Questions like these, and many others, will certainly have to be addressed, prayed about and discerned. As the Spirit of Jesus continues to rule the church, one thing is certain. A zebra mentality cannot rule.

Perhaps some of the zebra characteristics are in all of us. Only when we become convinced ourselves that Jesus came for all will we help the zebra change his "my way or no way, black and white mentality." A parish will grow not through my ideas or ways, but when all of God's people gather around the Table of the Lord and enflesh the Word of God, who welcomes all and loves all unconditionally.

What makes one believe their way of thinking is the only way? Certainly, it seems arrogant to think God blest one with full knowledge of His ways. Is it what pastors, associates, pastoral ministers, or presidents of organizations have so often encountered: "This is the way we've always done it!" Or is it a fear of change that closes the zebra to how God and His Spirit are working in the church? On a psychological level, is there an insecurity which causes one to always have to be right? Or finally, was one constantly put down that he or she has to prove their worth by proving their way is the only way?

As we mentioned earlier in this chapter, the zebra is committed to his church and believes passionately in his convictions. Is one final reason the zebra is the way he is (black and white) because he feels his church is being attacked? Elements of the church believe it is time for a married clergy; others are convinced it is time for women to be ordained priests; and still others would like to see those who have left the active ministry be reinstated. A zebra mentality views all of these as heresies and will feel a call to defend his church. Perhaps, however, it is time we realize that Jesus and His Spirit can take care of the church. Maybe our role is not so much to defend the church from our perceived heresies but to be open to the directions God is moving the church and to proclaim Jesus to one another.

We, too, at times, need to take on those zebra characteristics as we minister and proclaim Jesus within our society. We are told to just follow our feelings ("If it feels good, it's okay"). We also have our throw-away culture which does away with life, either through abortion or euthenasia. If you don't feel someone is useful—get rid of him or her. Jesus says very strongly in Mark 8:38: "Whoever is ashamed of me and of my words in this faithless and sinful generation, the Son of Man will be ashamed of when he comes in his Father's glory with the holy angels." Perhaps in these issues, and many others, we need a zebra mentality to stand up for our God, no matter what the cost.

Zebras do not travel in big herds. You never see a large number of zebras together—only small groups of twenty-five or thirty. When I saw those zebras in my first nightmare, I ran to my parents to spend the rest of the evening sleeping between them. The next morning I was okay. I could get up, go to school and play baseball once again. Being in the middle of the two people who gave me life provided me great strength. Is it not safe to say that the Eucharist, as the center of our lives and our praying communities, must be that to which we turn to in the challenging, and yet exciting, times that await us as we minister to and with one another?

We can never just turn to those who agree with us. Our energy cannot stem from those who only confirm our beliefs. Just as I found peace and renewed life by being with the two people who gave me life during the fears of my nightmare, we pray the zebra will turn to the Body of Christ and what God is calling it to through His Word, Jesus' teachings and the Traditions of the Church.

After twenty-seven years of parish ministry, I can say my early childhood nightmare still occurs in my ministry. Sometimes I, as all ministers have experienced, have been attacked by zebras for a decision made or the implementation of a new policy. On other occasions, I took on a zebra mentality at a meeting to "straighten them out!" Undoubtedly, this has occurred in many offices, marriages and family settings and neither scenario is beneficial to anyone involved. However, once our faith journey leads to a greater understanding of God's Word, prayer, and the Eucharist, we see the length and width of the table of Jesus and find ourselves in a win-win situation rather than a win-lose, "I'm right, you're wrong, end of discussion!"

In the late seventies, eighties and early nineties, a program entitled "Christ Renews His Parish" was very prominent in the Diocese of Cleveland. After every renewal, those who made the weekend would form a new team and ask The Spirit's guidance to choose their lay director or directress. I always approached that particular meeting believing I knew who should be the next director/directress. The amusing thing, however, is that whether it was a mens,' womens,' or youth renewal, the one whom I thought best for that role was never the person the Spirit of Jesus directed the rest of the group to choose. Always, without exception, the Spirit's choice would lead an excellent renewal.

Funny, isn't it? God's ways are always better than ours!

CHAPTER 9

THE SQUIRREL

Whisky frisky hippity hop
Up he goes to the treetop!
Whirly, twirly, round & round
Down he scampers to the ground.
Source Unknown

When I was ordained in 1972, the second Vatican council and its documents were beginning to unravel in parish life. I had been trained in much of the theology of the council and felt that at last the church would be saved by my Vatican II theology. In fact, I thought the people at my first assignment would be saved by August, after only three months of my assignment. How could they ever resist all of the gems and ideas I had? How could they not finally see the light by what I was going to show them? The church had existed for over 1900 years and now I, with my Vatican II theology and ideas, was going to finally save it and set it straight.

Never mind that Jesus had saved the church through his death and resurrection almost two thousand years earlier. Never mind that the grace of God is what saves us. I, with all of my new pearls of wisdom, with all kinds of new committees, with grandiose perceptions of getting some never heard of organization going, with a thousand ideas of how a parish should be run (even though the pastor at my first assignment had 20 years of experience), I was going to save the church. The savior of the church and world had come and I was he. Finally the church would have its answer.

As I reflect on those early years, I often ask myself what I was going to do after August once the church had been saved with all this new theology. Retire at the ripe old age of twenty-seven? Not a bad idea but as someone once said, "If you want to make God laugh, tell him your plans!"

When I think of the squirrel as one of the animals that came off the ark after the flood, I am often reminded of the times I am out jogging. Often I see a squirrel and want to go up to him and talk. (I guess some of my nephew is rubbing off on me). But the squirrel always runs swiftly and quickly away to avoid any contact with me. He runs here, there and everywhere getting food for himself. He sees a human and runs from intelligent life. It seems the squirrel tries to get food wherever he can, but, when approached, off he goes. He jumps from the pole to the ground, from the ground to a tree, from branch to branch, often seeming to run in a hundred different directions. And again, always away from intelligent life.

A squirrel does not get involved with others. Despite all their movements and running they will not converse with intelligent life. They can leap to places five times their height and flatten themselves out to get through narrow spaces, but always getting food for just themselves.

I would picture the squirrel in the parish similar to my first year after ordination. Just as I knew what was "best" for the parish without even asking about its history or traditions, the squirrel seems to be that person who has ideas to get everything started without ever having consulted "intelligent life." Like myself in those early years, they have all the answers, and know which programs or organizations must become part of parish life without ever having identified or listened to the actual needs of the parish. But don't worry! He'll get the people you need and "if you need me for anything, Father, I'll be there!"

One of the things that amazes me about the squirrel is how they flatten themselves out. As they run about they seem to be involved with so much, and, as we said earlier, move quickly from here to there. As they walk on wires I often wonder how they stay alive up there. Like a cat they seem to have a number of lives. In their running about they seem to say I need this, that and the other thing.

For one reason or another the squirrel in a parish wants to be involved in so much, often with the best of intentions. What is lacking, however, is that their personal preferences often are not conformed to the needs of the parish and, unfortunately, are not rooted in prayer. And when a parish is trying to move in one direction and the squirrel has other things on his plate he, like the squirrel outdoors, can simply "flatten out." One of the signs of the "flattening out" in the parish is when you call them for something they wanted to get started; suddenly you discover you cannot count on them. They "flatten out." And if they "flatten out" there can often be a period where they will sulk because they had all these ideas but no one seemed interested or wanted to buy into them. If they jump to another branch, it is again, with good intentions; however, because they have failed to see what is best for the community, through prayer, the same results are often reenacted.

Holy Redeemer Parish, an Italian congregation, located in the Collinwood area of the city of Cleveland, was my first assignment and because of their ethnicity, they had a strong devotion to St. Anthony. As a result, every June there were services and a novena to him. My initial thought was, "Well, that's all fine and dandy, but wait until they get a dose of some of my new theology. When they learn the way prayer services can be, they'll really learn how to pray!"

Talk about pride. Talk about arrogance. Talk about self-righteousness. There it was! Elderly people who had built the church in that area, who believed in the power of prayer, especially the power of intercessory prayer, and I was going to do away with that! Wow! Did I "flatten out" – and rightly so!

Today, some twenty-seven years later, no one believes more in the nine-day novena to our patron saint, Saint John Neumann, than I. As I have mentioned in other part of this book, the miracles and healings that have come about through his intercession are awesome and a copy of that novena is at the end of this book. I highly recommend it to all.

I ask again, as I have for many of the animals discussed, how can a minister, how can a parish grow, and how can one personally mature without centering himself or their faith community around prayer and the Eucharist? As a squirrel hastily moves about for acorns and nuts to sustain itself, so, we too, in all our moving about during our lives, can only exist and find peace through that great gift of Eucharist and our own personal daily prayer life. Part of Eucharist is that God calls us into relationship with Him and others through the death and resurrection of Jesus.

> "One of the scribes, when he came forward and heard them disputing and saw how well he had answered them, asked him, 'Which is the first of all the commandments?' Jesus replied, 'The first is this: "Hear, O Israel! The Lord our God is Lord alone! You shall love the Lord your God with all your heart, with all your soul, with all your mind, and with all your strength." The second is this: "You shall love your neighbor as yourself." There is no other commandment greater than these'" (Mark 12:28-31)

No one can grow in isolation apart from others or just saying the church needs various things and then fail to discuss them with the community. How often we hear someone say, "I pray on my own and I don't need a church!" The squirrel can think only of itself as it stores up its food. When we consider only our needs and isolate ourselves from the community we hinder our growth as well as that of the community. As we mentioned earlier, a squirrel has great intentions; but part of his time needs to discuss his thoughts with others to see if this is truly where God is leading the faith community. The squirrel seems to "know better than God" because he skips prayerful discernment and goes to what "he thinks best" when we all know that "The Father knows best!"

I have often reflected back on those early years, where I was then, and how I have seen the power of God work through me in my ministry, now, as pastor. Through the ministry of others to me, I have seen that as a time of growth many of us go through. In short, a time of insecurity. But when you rely on yourself, more than prayer, God's Word, and the gift of Eucharist, you are obviously going to fail. And fail because we see ourselves as "god" rather than a child of the God who loves us simply because we are His son or daughter, despite our failings and weaknesses. In the early ministry of Jesus we read:

> "It happened in those days that Jesus came from Nazareth of Galilee and was baptized in the Jordan by John. On coming up out of the water he saw the heavens being torn open and the Spirit, like a dove, descending upon him. And a voice came from the heavens, 'You are my beloved Son; with you I am well pleased'." (Mk. 1:9-11)

A teacher is said to have had a difficult time with one of her third grade students. However, she knew report card time was coming and figured that when the parents saw how bad the boy's grades were, he would undoubtedly get a lecture from them. When the boy brought his report card back signed the next day, she asked him what his parents had to say to him about his grades. The boy looked at her and replied, "Dad said someone is in trouble for those bad grades I got, so you'd better be careful!"

When confronted by the squirrel, that story comes to mind. Ministers of the parish and parishioners will be responsible for any failures in programs all because the squirrel wanted them started without any prayerful discernment There's a thousand programs to begin. The squirrel presents great ideas, but fails to get people to do the work. And, as I mentioned earlier, when you are insecure and are looking for people to validate your existence, it is a lot easier to expect others to take the initiative. If the program fizzles out the squirrel thus does not have to be held accountable. And when the program does fail the squirrel sulks. Just as my new programs and ideas "flattened out," in my first assignment, so, too, the squirrel, in parish life, will start to run about presenting new ideas since it is important to prove to himself and others that "he or she is a good minister!" In effect, however, they are only trying to prove something to themselves rather than ministering to the needs of the community.

Sometimes, in their running about, and to prove a point, the squirrel will call for a vote on something to show the majority desires what he wants. A parish community has to remember that the church is not a democracy. It is based on the gospel message of Jesus and His Father's Kingdom. There are certainly various ways to run an institution; for example, dictatorship, bureaucracy, autocracy, and democracy. And then there is the collaborative approach of the staff, who, through their commitment and leadership in prayer, in conjunction with the prayer of the community as it gathers around the Eucharist, discerns with God's people where Jesus and His Spirit are leading them. Just because the majority feel something should happen in parish life does not necessarily mean the parish should move in that direction. All decisions must flow from prayer, which at times may not be a majority decision; prayer, however, is always gospel-centered. In addition, the needs of not only the local parish community have to be considered, but, the diocese and universal church as well.

The interesting thing about a squirrel is that it focuses in on one thing—food. And maybe that's where we can learn something from him. He can help us understand and come to a greater realization that we, too, should have one objective: Jesus and how Jesus can be the true source of our strength and vision in our lives and in a parish setting. The squirrel does it hurriedly. But discerning and seeing where the Spirit is leading the church takes time. It takes a process. It takes patience. It takes prayer. It takes coming to know Jesus in His Body and Blood. The squirrel wants his food right now and so all parishioners must immediately do what he thinks is needed. How much, how fast can I get it.

In a way the squirrel might be in parishes because of our culture that demands instant gratification. I once saw a man waiting in the drive-through for breakfast with a cell phone in one hand and an electric razor in the other. Eat and run, on the move, from one meeting to another, one call to another, one fax to another, answer this pager, respond to that e-mail, accumulate so many miles for a free trip, give me the bottom line. The squirrel's bottom line is food; the parish needs to understand that it's bottom line is the Eucharistic meal and prayer—and that takes time, because of individual and communal prayer that is an integral part of this process.

Just as all my new programs and ideas for running a parish at Holy Redeemer were lacking in personal and communal prayer, so, too, programs, committees and ideas without prayer and the Eucharist have little to contribute to community life.

I was convinced starting a baptismal program would save the parish. Providing lector workshops would give us liturgies like we never experienced before. And what about a Liturgy Committee? And then if I got a contemporary guitar group started—wow! That would dazzle the people and the parish would be saved.

And once everyone experienced one of my great paraliturgical services how could they not shout out: "Jesus is Lord!" Finally, once again, if I may boldly proclaim, I, the savior had come.

But you see the fallacy? Without prayerful discernment, nothing—nothing can save a parish. All must focus on prayer and the Eucharist. The leadership and example must come from the staff itself and the individuals on the staff. If prayer is not something that the staff (clergy, religious and lay) live, how can they expect their people in the community to have a foundation in prayer?

Besides the prayer of the professional staff, it is important times are set aside for the secretaries, bookkeeper, support staff to take days of recollection. Do household and support staff take time at least weekly for communal prayer? It's okay if someone calls between 11:30 a.m. and 12:00 noon and hears the recording that no one is available at this time because the staff is at prayer. If anything, it shows where the focus of the parish is.

As I look back on my first assignment, perhaps some of those ideas would have come to fruition if prayer would have been more a part of my life. Saint Paul says it so eloquently in 1 Corinthians where we read:

> "But I shall show you a still more excellent way. If I speak in human and angelic tongues but do not have love, I am a resounding gong or a clashing cymbal. And if I have the gift of prophecy and

comprehend all mysteries and all knowledge; if I have all faith so as to move mountains, but do not have love, I am nothing. If I give away everything I own, and if I hand my body over so that I may boast, but do not have love, I gain nothing." (1 Cor. 12:31a-13:3)

　　Maybe we all need the experience of being a squirrel like I was in my first assignment. Playing, believing I was God, having all the answers, starting lots of programs, running here and there, jumping from one wire to another with new committees, and then sulking because nobody bought into them. How could they? The ideas weren't coming from prayer and parish discernment. I had come. Yet only when God comes into a life is one saved.

　　Whether it came through my reading or the tapes I have listened to, I cannot recall. But somewhere, I remember hearing or reading the following: "The young man who has never cried is a savage and the old man who has never laughed is a fool." I like this and believe it says a lot. Whether we are an accountant, lawyer, a nurse, teacher, financial consultant, in the medical profession, a priest, religious, or pastoral minister, we all begin with high ideals. It's part of the process. To take ourselves so seriously that we believe we have all the answers is to become a savage. We expect things from others to make programs fit our ideals. We demand others meet our needs. On the other hand, to grow old and not laugh at our weaknesses and failures also hinders growth, as it in only in admitting them that God can begin to work through us.

　　Perhaps we have to ignore the squirrel inside. We have to set aside that part of us that thinks I have all the answers and turn to God, to His son Jesus, and to the gift of Eucharist that he offers each of us. In the end, I'd like to tell the squirrel: "Lighten up and see the entire creation of God. You're just one part of the entire plan of God!"

In 1995-96, the parishioners of Saint John Neumann Parish built the new activity center, meeting rooms, gymnasium and kindergarten which I referred to in the beginning of the chapter on The Badger. One evening, as I locked the church, I stood in the activity center and thought, "These people have a lot to be proud of! They have a very nice new building!"

Then I recalled, for whatever reason, how upset I was when the air-conditioning units came three days late, the floor people were here four extra days, and how I took that anger out on others. Then it struck me: will anyone care about that a year from now? Does anyone discuss those issues today? Will anyone give a darn about that five years from now?

We all know the answer, but because we can get so wound up in our own little world we sometimes forget it. The squirrel teaches us to grow a brain that allows us to see we need involvement with others, and not just ourselves! Ideas and programs of how a parish should be run will never save people. What will save them is how I witness Jesus in my life and that witness can only begin to develop as I come to know Jesus through prayer and Eucharist. As I, ministers, and support staff, of a parish, grow in prayer and witness so, too, will people in the various groups and committees also come to know Jesus. Because of that, the parish cannot help but grow.

Over the last year or so I was involved with two ten year-old twins, both of whom received heart transplants within a period of four months. After visiting one of them one summer evening at Cleveland Clinic, Fred asked me if I would pray with him. I said I had planned to do that and so we started to pray. When I finished, Fred mentioned he had become good friends with a 12 year old boy from Michigan and asked if I would go with him to pray with his new acquaintance. And so the two of us went and prayed with his friend and family.

Later, driving home, I thought what a witness this ten year-old boy had given. First, he asked for prayer and thoroughly believed in it. Secondly, he asked me to pray with another. How many adults would do the same? And thirdly, he continues to pray thorough the intercession of Saint John Neumann, whom I am convinced has been an integral part of the healing power of God, touching him and his brother.

You see, it was not ideas, programs, or new theology that brought the Lord to another. Rather Fred brought Jesus to me because he believed with great faith and hope that the power of God can bring healing. I thank God and praise God everyday for the witness of Fred and his brother.

Three months after arriving at Saint John Neumann, I called the parish together to develop a vision statement. With the help of the Diocesan Pastoral Planning Office we discussed what we appreciated about St. John's, what was going on or not going on that concerned us, and what our hopes for the parish were. After a number of initial gatherings, we had a Steering Committee to follow-up. At one of the assemblies, and I will never forget this, a woman said, "You know, father, when people come here to this church for meetings, they should not be like their work meetings during the day. They should be different—not bottom line, end result stuff, but meetings that are different. They should begin with prayer and they should have a sense of prayer about them!"

After hearing that statement, there was no doubt in my mind that people are really looking for, and desiring, the Lord Jesus in their lives! How important it was for me to feed them and for them to feed me. Because of that initial convocation and that woman's comment we began meetings with more than just a ten second prayer. Parish council would spend thirty minutes in prayer before the meeting, sharing scripture, praying for the parish, and spending time in silence. At a recent staff meeting some commented on how people in the parish seem comfortable, during prayer, with silence, recognizing that it is often in silence that God speaks to us. At times, we feel we have to fill in the silence and speak, but again, that can go back to the "squirrel mentality" where you talk to alleviate the discomfort you feel with yourself.

That remark about parish meetings being different from regular work meetings said a lot. And yet, how can we begin to bring that to our meetings if we are flying around from one program to another without the direction of Jesus coming from prayer. Just as the squirrel is searching for food, we, too, have to look for Jesus in our life.

Someone told me: When you look at your shadow in the morning, as the sun begins to rise in the east, it is very big. But as you approach mid-day, the shadow is much smaller.

Isn't that what our lives should be. Perhaps when we are young and have all the answers, we see ourselves in a pretty big way. But, hopefully, as we grow older we see less and less of our shadow, less and less of ourselves, and more and more of God, who is Light, overcoming the darkness of self and sin. How can God be witnessed and shared with others when there is no room within ourselves to take Him in, all because we are filled up with ourselves?

Call me strange, but I'd love (just once) to talk to a squirrel when I'm out running. I'd like to tell him to "slow down! Somehow the Lord will provide." If we're His children we're all He has. Daily, finish one thing that is truly "prayer-centered" and not "self-centered."

Let the squirrels jump from one thing to another, but for me, it's a lot better to have found out that the only life that I can live is the one that finds Jesus in prayer. Only then can I start to share Jesus with others and begin to center a parish and staff around Jesus and the Eucharist. It is that which is central for me.

CHAPTER 10

THE PELICAN

During the course of this book I have alluded several times to an eleven week institute for priests that I attended during the fall of 1994 in Rome. The continuing education office of the Diocese of Cleveland sends one priest each spring and fall to The North American College and the experience is undoubtedly among the top five of my life. Approximately forty priests from the United States studied with me and four of us still get together every October.

My first Sunday at the institute provided me with an experience I often find myself reflecting upon. On that particular Sunday, a number of us went to St. Peter's Basilica, located about five minutes from the college, to concelebrate their 10:30 a.m. mass.

As we walked through the crowds and approached St. Peter's, I remember hearing a number of people speaking various languages. Some were rather obvious, Italian, Spanish, Polish, English,

Slovak, and German. And then there were those that were not so obvious. But somehow they were all headed for the same destination—Saint Peter's Basilica and the 10:30 a.m. mass.

During the mass I was sitting on the side of the sanctuary as the mass began in Italian. When we reached the Word of God, the first reading was read in a language that went right over my head. The second reading, also, was in a different tongue, and, like the first, unrecognizable. Finally the gospel was proclaimed in Latin and I was able to understand some phrases from my Latin background during my seminary education.

The homily was delivered in Italian. By that time I had mastered "buon giorno," "prego," "gratie," and "quanto!" Not bad for five days in Rome, but hardly enough to understand what the priest was saying. After the 12 minute homily, we moved to the profession of faith, in Italian, and seven petitions delivered in seven various languages, one of which was English. The language of the Eucharistic prayer escapes my memory. However, it was either Latin or Italian and the hymns were sung in various native tongues.

Although I am not one to do a lot of journal writing, I remember writing down some thoughts that had struck me.

Why were these people there? Many of those present, like me, wondered what was being said. I reflected on how many people understood the homily. How many were aware of what was being said during the Eucharistic prayer? How many recognized the petitions, especially if in an unfamiliar language? And what about those who heard no familiar language at all?

And yet, these people of various cultures, backgrounds and languages came together as one because of The Body and Blood of Jesus Christ. Eucharist! They were celebrating the life, death and resurrection of Jesus! It didn't matter if you were a rabbit, zebra, raccoon, badger, dog, hyena, skink, kangaroo or a squirrel. What was important was that we shared and celebrated Eucharist, together, as one body of Jesus.

This was especially evident to me during the Our Father, which was prayed in Latin (Pater Noster, qui est in caelis...) and the sign of peace. Somehow, we all knew we were praying together to our loving and forgiving Father, our one Father. Somehow we were aware that we were participating in the peace of Jesus with one another.

Wow! The unifying power of Eucharist. The gathering of people of all races and nationalities in prayer. The love of Jesus which all these people had experienced. The forgiveness of God which all had received in their lives. The healing power of Jesus that touched so many. The hope that Jesus had been to so many. The thanksgiving so many must have had for a great variety of God's gifts in their lives through their various cultures and races. The awareness these people, from all over the world, felt. Despite any pain and agony that might have been a part of their lives, their faith led them to celebrate the fact that God never abandons His people.

Undoubtedly, many of those people present that day had great accomplishments and achievements they could be proud of; and many probably had respectable positions in the corporate world. There were probably some with athletic achievements and trophies, some who were in poverty and others who had no family. But somehow, they all knew nothing has meaning without the Body and Blood of Jesus. As Jesus said in the Gospel of Saint John:

> "Amen, Amen, I say to you, unless you eat the flesh of the Son of Man and drink his blood, you do not have life within you. Whoever eats my flesh and

drinks my blood has eternal life, and I will raise him on the last day. For my flesh is true food, and my blood is true drink. Whoever eats my flesh and drinks my blood remains in me and I in him." (Jn. 6:53-56)

Do you remember the scene in Mark's gospel where the disciples came back to Jesus and tell Him all that they had accomplished?

"He went around to the villages in the vicinity teaching. He summoned the Twelve and began to send them out two by two and gave them authority over unclean spirits... So they went off and preached repentance. They drove out many demons, and they anointed with oil many who were sick and cured them... The apostles gathered together with Jesus and reported all they had done and taught. He said to them; 'Come away by yourselves to a deserted place and rest a while'... so they went off in the boat by themselves to a deserted place." (Mk. 6:6b-7,12-13, 30-31a,32).

Jesus responds by taking them to a deserted place in the desert to be at prayer with His Father. He was speaking to all of us in the zoos of our parishes, too. If we do not take time to focus ourselves solely on God, we will always be busy, active, reaching out for things to do. We may even think it is because of us that good things are happening in our lives rather than the power of God. However, in the end, we will be pitied "like sheep without a shepherd." (Mt. 9:36b) We will only be giving ourselves and not

Jesus. And we will be pitied because we think our strength is in ourselves, when, in reality, it is from God.

We don't need to tell people what we have done—we need to show what God has done in and through each and every one of us. It would have been interesting to hear from those at St. Peter's how God had touched their lives. We would have seen the power of God as far as the ends of the earth.

Activity! Activity! Activity! Our parish and business lives often center around activities and meetings, which, at times, are necessary and very beneficial. Unfortunately, we can often substitute such things for prayer. We start a program, initiate this committee, or begin a new organization to get people involved. But without prayer and Eucharist, we wander like sheep without a shepherd, and Jesus becomes someone I use in "my parish" rather than the foundation of His church.

The pelican gives her blood—do we not have a far greater gift to unite and strengthen our parishes in the Body and Blood of Jesus in the gift of Eucharist? How can we give less than Jesus?

After discussing the previous nine animals that came off Noah's ark, it is appropriate we conclude our journey of the zoo with the pelican. Unlike the other animals, we will look only at its redemptive side. Although I was not aware of it before writing this book, I was told by my associate, Fr. David Trask, that the pelican is a wonderful symbol of Eurcharist. Upon further research, it was one of a number of animals that interested St. Augustine (cf Saint Augustine of Hippo, Essays dealing with his Life and Times and some features of his work by the Very Reverend Father Hugh Pope, O.P., S.T.M., D.S.S.)

The pelican is not an animal obvious to us in America since it lends itself more to Egypt. However, while there were a number of animals that were of interest to Augustine, among them the owl, eagle and sparrow, it seems the pelican, especially, lent itself to his reflection. He pointed out how the mother pelican will kill her offspring with blows from her bill and then finds herself mourning over the dead bodies in the nest for three days. Further observation showed how she would inflict wounds on herself and then pour her blood on her children so that they came to life once again.

Did not Jesus give Himself, His own body and blood, so that we, too, might share life with one another and eventually eternal life with God.? Just as the pelican nourishes her young with her flesh and blood, as a last resort, so that they will not starve, so, too, is the death of Jesus on the cross—a last resort to show us how much His Father loves and forgives us.

In my experience of the liturgy at St. Peter's, the people felt a sense of unity with God and one another. Is not the call into relationship with one another and with God the call of parish life?

Part of the eleven week institute in Rome included a ten day journey to the Holy Land. Like the studies in Rome, this was also a tremendous, gratifying experience. We visited a number of sites, one of which was called the Upper Room. It is interesting to note that on a pillar in the Upper Room in Jerusalem is a symbol of the pelican. In addition, it is also on the tabernacle door at the church of the Agony of the Garden in Jerusalem. In our own Cathedral of St. John's, in Cleveland, a pelican carving can be found at the base of the altar.

In The Oxford Dictionary of the Christian Church, edited by F.L. Cross, Oxford University Press, the pelican is discussed in the following way:

> PELICAN. The image of the Pelican, "vulning herself" with her beak to feed her young with her blood, has been widely used in Christian symbolism

> to typify the Lord's redeeming work, esp. as mediated through the Blessed Sacrament. Well-known instances are the first line of the 6th stanza of "Adoro te devote," and the figure of the pelican on the column in the quadrangle of Corpus Christi College, Oxford. At Durham the Blessed Sacrament used to be reserved in a silver Pelican suspended over the high altar. (page 1059)

Just as Augustine reflected on the pelican, we need to ponder on the gift of Eucharist and God's forgiveness in our lives and in our daily prayer. Jesus knew how busy our lives can be, and we need to heed his advice to go off to a deserted place and pray.

One of the things that amazes me when I travel on an airplane is to see the luggage that comes on a plane, the so-called "carry on luggage!" It's amazing to sit and watch people try to jam oversized and overstuffed baggage into the overhead compartments and under seats. It's interesting to see them get upset when the flight attendant informs them that they will have to check their carry on baggage and claim it after the flight.

There's a lot of excess luggage that all of us carry into parish life. We have our own upbringings, our family life, our religious backgrounds, our needs, our wants, our hopes, our aspirations, our "egos!" All these are a part of the zoo. But somehow there has to be something or someone to unite us; to give us the healing we need. Will it be the media or television that all too often seems to glamorize the sensational? Or will it be movies that fill our minds with so much violence and illicit and immoral behavior? Will it be the revenge we seek, when we desire to get even, only to know we're still not at peace?

Is it only in the values that give us hope? Is it only in the virtues that guide our thoughts and actions? Is it only in the goals that direct us? What will it be beyond this?

Is the answer in the Eucharistic symbol of the pelican, who displays for us what Jesus did? It is Jesus who gave us His Body and Blood in the Eucharist! It is Jesus who calls us, as one, into prayer! It is Jesus who wants us in relationship with Him and one another.

One of the fascinating things of priesthood is dealing with couples preparing for the sacrament of marriage. They come from different backgrounds which can substantially affect their relationship together as husband and wife. Probably my greatest pain in these situations is that often they spend the last nine to twelve months of their engagement preparing for the "perfect wedding!" Society puts a lot of pressure (as can parents) to have the wedding of the century. Activity, activity, activity! As a result they stop growing together.

Sooner or later one will say to me "I thought I knew him (her) but I guess I didn't! I never saw that side of him until we were married!"

There is no perfect parish; no perfect pastor or associate pastor; no perfect staff or deacon; no perfect marriage; and no perfect organization or parishioner. Jesus offered the perfect sacrifice to His Father, and our Father, for our sins. On the other hand there will never be a perfect liturgy as all of us are imperfect animals.

However, we are called to be faithful to God in our personal prayer and when we celebrate Eucharist. We must remain faithful to prayer and to centering our parishes around Eucharist; if we do not, one of the animals of the zoo will prevail and wear us out. They will want perfection "as they see it to be" rather than open themselves to Jesus and His Spirit as it manifests itself through the animals around the Table of the Lord.

We cannot believe in someone we do not know; nor can we center our parishes around someone we have not come to know if all we do is allow the animals of the zoo to predominate and be the center of parish life. Just as people with various addictions often "bottom out," and realize they have to turn to a higher power, sooner or late we will have nothing to give if we do not share the Body and Blood of Jesus. The Body and Blood that absorbs our suffering and pain and transforms it into new life gives us hope for the future because of God's promise to never abandon His people.

We need people within our parish communities to witness to the gift of Eucharist. We need parishioners who stand up in a world that is so fragile and fleeting and passing away. We need them to say, "Don't you understand! Your pursuit of happiness is not in what you hear on television; it is not in the malls; it's not in your addictions; it's not in the latest book of a talk show guest; it's not in drugs or fleeting sexual encounters. Rather, peace and joy and the fulfillment of life come from the Body and Blood of Jesus Christ."

In a sense, it's the difference between management and leadership. It seems the management of a company was in a jungle looking for the enemy and brought some knives to fight them. Then they voted to hire someone to sharpen the knives; next, some in management said we'll need a person to keep the sharpener healthy; and so they hired a nutritionist. And if we do that, another management person suggested, we'd better get a doctor on the payroll; finally, they decided to organize a committee to put all this together.

In the midst of all of this, someone climbed a tree, reached it's top and yelled out, "Hey, you know what? We're in the wrong jungle!"

Perhaps we need leaders like that in our parish communities. More than the management of the world, which continues to pollute our minds with, "the ten ways to happiness," and other such remedies for the loneliness so many experience, we need leaders who show us we're simply in the wrong jungle when we buy into the world and not the Body and Blood of Jesus.

And thank God there are so many who bring that promise to others in parish life, who truly feed of the Body and Blood of Jesus and accept His death and resurrection as a sign of new life. A great number give of themselves to bring back the hurt and alienated. Many have given of themselves to make their parishes what they are today. Thousands throughout the country teach and witness to Jesus in PSR classes, while some share their music talents. Others believe God has called them to proclaim God's Word, and there are those who give of themselves through their daily prayer, whether that be praying with others in the church, telephone prayer chains or devoting an hour during the week praying for the parish in front of the Blessed Sacrament. Many pray the rosary in parishes to seek the intercession of Mary, while thousands throughout a diocese find time to celebrate daily Mass.

In addition to these, parishioners give of their time in the various diocesan youth ministries and there are those who minister in their professional lives in ways that will never be known. All of these understand the symbol of the pelican, that for life to come about, they must at times give of themselves.

Yes, there are sinners within the church, myself included; and, like many institutions, the church has not been spared of scandals among the clergy, religious and lay people. However, there also have been tremendous saints, many of whom are within our own parish boundaries, who allow that symbol of the pelican to be the guide in their lives and the Body and Blood of Jesus to lead them on their faith journey.

Many of us talk of how things need to be different in the church today. I know that I am just as good as the other in complaining about certain situations. And I know that so many times there seem to be such simple solutions to the various issues confronting our universal church as well as on a diocesan and local level. Certainly, we can never cut off dialogue on how God's Spirit is moving us as church. And yet I have come to realize there are some things that don't have an answer and will be the first of a number of questions I plan on asking God when I meet Him. It is at times like these, when there are more questions than answers, when circumstances in our lives do not make sense, that I ask myself: can anything substitute for the Body and Blood of Jesus and the prayer of the faith community?

Back in the seventies, I remember a book entitled "I'm OK, You're OK!" by Thomas A. Harris. I often wonder if someone should have written a book "I'm Not Ok and That's Ok!" <u>No parish is ok</u> and every parish has all the animals. And every parish has sinners, people who have hurt one another, disappointments, people who have done dumb and stupid things; and every parish is in need of healing. We're not ok but you know what? <u>That's ok!</u> But because we have the Body and Blood of Jesus to unite us as a parish, and because we can come together in prayer through Jesus, with Jesus and in Jesus, we can proclaim hope to one another that it can be different. We can own our hurts, our pain and find new life through the reconciliation of Jesus, who gave of His own flesh, on the cross. The good news is that Jesus is the Bread of Life and the Bread of Life that is present in every parish.

The Eucharist, Jesus Himself, has given us so much—His own Body and Blood so that we can feed off of Him and feed one another in our parish life together. One of the most difficult things, as we mentioned when discussing the kangaroo, is to let go to God and to His Son, Jesus. If only we could learn that in our zoos.

Many years ago, in my spiritual reading, I recall reading a meditation about hands and it has always remained with me. To this day, I always like to share it with parishioners on the feast of Corpus Christi.

The thought expressed was that everyone of us comes into this world with fists clenched. Probably one who is a parent can appreciate that more than I, as they see their child emerge from the mother's womb. However, when I do see a newly-born infant I often look at their little fists and how they are closed. On the other hand, the article expressed how we also die with open hands. Whenever I have been with a person when they passed away or prayed with the family while we were in the presence of the body, I have observed the deceased with open hands.

What tremendous symbolism! We struggle each and every second of our existence to open our hands to the graces and the power of God in our life. We hold on to so many things we believe will bring us security, but, in the end, it is only when we open those clenched hands to God that we find true freedom. We should certainly pray for the grace to discern what we hold onto that prevents us and our parish communities from finding the love and forgiveness of God with open hands.

When I first found out of the possibility of going to Rome, I was a little hesitant. Luckily, at that time, I was going to visit a good priest friend of mine in Buffalo, Father Joe Gatto. I mentioned to Joe, who had studied in Rome, of the possibility but shared some concerns. "Like what?" Joe asked "Well, there's this and that," I said, and "that and this, and a few other things!" "Nonsense!" Joe countered. "You 're just afraid of not being able to eat the foods you eat here, you're concerned whether you'll have your peanut butter and jelly and frosted flakes, whether you'll be able to play tennis and how you're going to live during the fall without football. You're afraid to let go of your securities. Get in the car! We're going to the bookstore to pick up a book on Italy and speaking the Italian language; and you're going to go!"

He was right. I didn't want to let go of my securities and I thank God Joe reminded me of this. If he hadn't, I would have closed myself to one of the greatest signs of God's presence in my life.

One of the things I enjoy doing, when on vacation, is to play a slot machine in a casino. I give myself a certain amount to lose and, win or lose, it doesn't matter. I just like sitting there, playing and being entertained. I get lost in my own little world. If I can make twenty dollars worth of quarters last three hours I'm happy.

It's fascinating to watch someone's reaction when the person sitting next to them leaves their machine. What immediately happens? The person next to it (myself included) drops a quarter into their machine. It seems like we never have enough. And when I leave my machine and someone immediately starts to play it, I watch (although I try to play it real smooth and act as if I'm not interested) to see if they win on the machine I was playing. (Actually, I pray they don't).

That whole scene tells me so much. We are never happy with the blessings we have all received. And we all have been given so much. Despite that, we always have to try another machine, another fad of the world. Secondly, why are we so hesitant to share God's goodness with others, especially when so many in our world our homeless, without food and in poverty? What reaction comes over us if somebody else wins on our machine?

To this day, I have never heard one person say at the end of his or her life that he or she wishes they would have worked one more day. I have seen people say, however, that they wish they would have loved more, taken additional time with their loved ones. I have heard them mention they wish they would have realized, "what was really important" and would have been more thankful for what they have. I have heard them say they should have spent more time with their children and shared more with them. And I have heard them say they wish they wouldn't have gotten so upset over so many little things that really are not that big of a deal.

What brought all those people together in Rome? Was it St. Peter's Basilica? Was it the city itself? Or were they all able to say Pater Noster qui est in caelis...because of the gift of Eucharist?

My brothers and sisters, God has given us so much in the Body and Blood of His Son, Jesus. It is all we need. It is a gift given freely, unearned by us, but nevertheless shared with us only because God is the loving, healing and forgiving God we are called to know and imitate. May we grow in our appreciation of His gift of Eucharist through our individual and communal prayer lives and may we share that great gift of Jesus in the Eucharist with others. Praise God.

SUMMARY

If we go back to our original story of Jesus at the fancy restaurant, many have probably found themselves sitting at the table of the Lord saying something similar to the following, "How can Bennie be here? He's such a hypocrite! If people only knew him as I do!" or "I saw Patti so rude the other day. From the way she acted I don't know how she could ever go to communion!" or "I'm surprised the church didn't crumble when Eric and Susan stepped inside. They haven't been here for years!" or "After seeing Don overindulge the other night and the way he acted you'd think he'd be ashamed to show his face in church!" and "If people only knew how John treats his family!"

Not only parishioners can have comments made about them, but statements about the priest celebrant or pastoral minister may be overheard, in the following manner, "The way Father talked to Mrs. Smith you'd think he'd be uneasy about celebrating Mass for us." "And the way Sister Ann blasted poor old Mrs. Jones, she has her nerve lecturing! What's this church coming to, anyway!"

In today's world there is a great deal of adulation given to rock stars, sports celebrities and movie stars. As a result many can often look up to such "heroes" as their leaders. But the real people who will influence our society are those who believe that the power of God can transform their lives, family and parish communities. And just as important, they live each and every day animated by the Holy Spirit. You and I, in our lives and parishes, are called to be that charismatic person, that is, energized by the Spirit of Jesus. We are Spirit-filled people who know and believe we are the church.

In the very first chapter of the bible, (Genesis 1:27) we read the following: "God created man in his image,/ in the divine image he created him;/ male and female he created them." To find out who we are then, it is essential we look to God rather than any of "society's heroes." As we come to know this God of ours through prayer, His Word, and through the Body and Blood of His Son, Jesus, we will be filled more with the transforming power of God's love.

To my knowledge, no one has ever been converted to the life, death and resurrection of Jesus through an encyclical, book, letter, church teaching, the commandments, or a homily. However, from my experience, I do believe many have come to know Jesus because they saw others, in their human weakness and sinfulness, give witness to the power of God.

We cannot be content on just saying I'm Catholic, I go to Church, I was raised Catholic. That'll never change anything. But if we, with all our anxieties, similar to the apostles in the upper room with all their fears and doubts, believe there is a greater power than ourselves in life, namely God, His son Jesus and His spirit, then we will take what we do around the altar on Sunday into our lives each and every day.

When we can fearlessly tell others that we believe in Jesus; when we can share with others that we trust in the power of prayer; when we can ask a waitress to pray with us at a meal without shame, when we can respond to someone who asks us for prayer with, "Let's pray right now!" then truly people understand the words of I John: "Beloved, if God so loved us, we also must love one another. No one has ever seen God. Yet, if we love one another, God remains in us, and his love is brought to perfection in us." (1 Jn. 4:11-12)

Often, when having been asked to pray with someone, I have done just what was mentioned above and responded with, "OK, let's pray right now!" They will respond with, "What?" "Well, you asked for prayer," I said, "So let's pray!"

When we believe in the teachings of Jesus, the traditions of the church, the inspired word of God, the forgiveness of Jesus, the healing power of Jesus, when we believe in the power of Eucharist, individually and as a praying community, when we believe in the Mass as a coming together, not because we profess to be holy, but because we believe in the power of Jesus in the Eucharist...then we are church!

When we can come to the table of the Lord and own the fact that we have our prejudices and brokeness; that we have a difficult time with so and so; that we have a difficult time with that type of animal; that we can't forgive as much as we would like to; when we can come and own our sins, then church begins to happen.

When Jesus appeared to Thomas on the evening of the resurrection. (Jn. 20:24-29) He showed him His wounds inflicted by the animals of his time. Perhaps when we come to view our own woundedness, in the light of God's forgiveness, we become church.

> "In giving this instruction, I do not praise the fact that your meetings are doing more harm than good. First of all I hear that when you meet as a church there are divisions among you, and to a degree I believe it; there have to be factions among you in order that [also] those who are approved among you may become known. When you meet in one place, then, it is not to eat the Lord's supper, for in eating, each one goes ahead with his own supper, and one goes hungry while another gets drunk. Do you not have houses in which you can eat and drink? Or do you show contempt for the church of God and make those who have nothing feel ashamed? What can I say to you? Shall I praise you? In this matter I do not praise you. For I received from the Lord what I also handed over to you, that the Lord Jesus, on the night he was handed on to you, that the Lord Jesus, on the night he was handed over, took bread, and after he had given thanks, broke it and said, 'This is

my body that is for you. Do this in remembrance of me.' In the same way also the cup, after supper, saying, 'This cup is the new covenant in my blood. Do this, as often as you drink it, in remembrance of me.' For as often as you eat this bread and drink the cup, you proclaim the death of the Lord until he comes." (1Cor.11:17-26)

A boy once went to summer camp for a week. His mother packed his clothes. When he returned he had three ribbons; one for swimming, one for the fastest in races and the third for the neatest packed bag when ready to return home. His mother was skeptical of the third award and asked him about it and how he got that reward since it wasn't his track record. "It was easy," he said. "I never unpacked it when I came."

God certainly packs an abundance of His love, forgiveness and healing, as well as the gift of Jesus and His Spirit, into our lives. However, we can be like the boy at camp and because of fear of what others will think never share the Lord of our life. It may be because of the animals that are in each and every one of us, or the lack of prayer and the lack of community that makes us self-centered and afraid to take the risk to share Jesus. God's life will come about when we unpack ourselves and open ourselves up to conversion. If we stay within ourselves, and our focus is: "I can do it by myself," conversion will probably never come about.

Conversion is only going to come about through relationships in our life, with and among each and every animal of the zoo. The conversion to build God's Kingdom of non-judgments, love, forgiveness and equality comes about through a relationship with God and others.

Do you remember the bombing in Oklahoma City in April of 1995? People were a little different immediately after that. Someone remarked how people weren't so snappy. Or I remember playing tennis the day after desert storm began in 1991. I felt guilty. I was enjoying a game and people faced the possibility of dying.

Somehow these experiences, and others similar to it, tell us we are in relationship with others. We realize others are just like us and our lives could end at any given moment. In the case of Oklahoma City, people in that Federal building were planning things, they were going to take their kid to a sports activity, a weekend get together, they were going to work and suddenly it ended. Any family could identify with them and enter into relationship with them, as could any individual. That bonding, if only for a while during those occurrences, brought about conversion.

There is a powerful event that I have often experienced in my priesthood. Occasionally I have been with a person who knows they are dying and they will tell me something similar to the following, "Father, I can't wait to die--I can't wait to be reunited with my spouse, my mom, my dad and see God!" What an act of faith, what an act of surrender! They tell us being united with others, loved ones and God, is the only essential element in life. Yes, they've lived with a lot of animals, and have been some of those animals, but ultimately to be united with family, friends, others and God is all that counts.

That conversion comes about in our lives, at times slowly, but when we realize we are part of the zoo and need the others in the zoo, and ultimately God, it happens.

And so, yes, it is the same zoo everywhere with different animals; but with gratitude we can all turn to the power of God and always say, "Christ has died, Christ is risen, and Christ will come again!" In the end we can be grateful because it is a God, who, in spite of us, continues to be with us on our journey of faith and our journey of conversion. It is the powerful God who will never abandon us, who has made us into His own image and likeness and continues to dwell among us, through Jesus, in the Eucharist. For this we can only say, "Amen! Come, Lord Jesus!" (Revelation 22:20b).

NOVENA PRAYERS

In Honor of

SAINT JOHN NEUMANN, C.SS.R.

NINE -DAY PRAYER
Imploring Saint John Neumann's Intercession

1st Day—

O Saint John Neumann, obtain for me a lively faith in all the truths that the Holy Roman Catholic Church teaches, together with the diving light to know the vanity of all earthly things, and the hideousness of my sins. Obtain for me, also the special favor which I now ask through your intercession with God.

Let us pray

O Lord, Who on earth both praised and practiced the hidden life, grant that, in these days of pride and outward display, the humble ways of Your Servant, Saint John Neumann, may inspire us to imitate Your divine example.

Teach us, O Divine Master, to be like Your servant, the holy bishop; intent on pleasing only You and on performing our good actions free from the desire to be seen and glorified by men.

That his holy example may influence an ever increasing number of souls, grant, O Lord, the favors we ask through his intercession. Amen.

N.B.—Say One Our Father, Hail Mary and Glory be to the Father, after each day's prayer.

2nd Day—

O Saint John Neumann, obtain for me the firm hope of receiving from God, through the merits of Jesus Christ and the intercession of Mary and your prayers the pardon of my sins, final perseverance and paradise. Obtain for me also the special favor which I now ask through your intercession with God.

Let us pray: O Lord, etc.

3rd Day—

O Saint John Neumann, obtain for me an ardent love of God, that will detach me from the love of created things and from myself, to love Him alone and to spend myself for His glory. Obtain for me also the special favor which I now ask through your intercession with God.

Let us pray: O Lord, etc.

4th Day—

O Saint John Neumann, obtain for me perfect resignation to the will of God, that I may accept in peace, sufferings, contempt persecutions, loss of goods, and reputation, and finally death itself. Obtain for me also the special favor which I now ask through your intercession with God.

Let us pray: O Lord, etc.

5th Day—

O Saint John Neumann, obtain for me a heartfelt sorrow for my sins, that I may never cease to weep over the displeasure I have given my God. Obtain for me also the special favor I now ask through your intercession with God.

Let us pray: O Lord, etc.

6th Day—
O Saint John Neumann, obtain for me a true love of my neighbor, that will make me do good even to those who have offended me. Obtain for me also the special favor which I now ask through your intercession with God.

Let us pray: O Lord, etc.

7th Day—
O Saint John Neumann, obtain for me the virtue of holy purity and the help required to resist impure temptations by invoking the holy names of Jesus and Mary. Obtain for me also the special favor which I now ask through your intercession with God.

Let us pray: O Lord, etc.

8th Day—
O Saint John Neumann, obtain for me a tender devotion to the Passion of Jesus Christ, to the Blessed Sacrament, and to my dear Mother, Mary. Obtain for me also the special favor which I now ask through your intercession with God.

Let us pray: O Lord, etc.

9th Day—
O Saint John Neumann, obtain for me above all the grace of final perseverance and the grace always to pray for it, especially in time of temptation and at the hour of death. Obtain for me also the special favor which I now ask through your intercession with God.

Let us pray: O Lord, etc.

PRAYER

O my God, I adore Your infinite Majesty with all the powers of my soul. I thank You for the graces and gifts which You bestowed upon Your faithful servant, Saint John Neumann. I ask You to glorify him also on earth. For this end I beseech You to grant me the favor which I humbly ask from Your Fatherly mercy. Amen.

(3 Our Fathers and 3 Hail Mary's)